Portugal!
thanks for attend-
PMC 2016 *Brian*

Ancient Faith
for the Modern World

A BRIEF GUIDE TO
THE APOSTLES' CREED

Brian Schmisek

DEDICATION

To my parents, John and Rita,
who sacrificed to send their children
to Catholic schools

ANCIENT FAITH FOR THE MODERN WORLD
A Brief Guide to the Apostles' Creed
Brian Schmisek

Design by Patricia A. Lynch

Published by ACTA Publications, 4848 N. Clark St.,
Chicago, IL 60640, (800) 397-2282, actapublications.com

Library of Congress Catalog Number: 2016933742
ISBN: 978-0-87946-571-1
Printed in the United States of America by Total Printing Systems
Year 25 24 23 22 21 20 19 18 17 16
Printing 12 11 10 9 8 7 6 5 4 3 2 First

♲ Text printed on 30% post-consumer recycled paper

Contents

How to Use This Book

This book is written primarily for Catholic school teachers, parish catechetical leaders, catechists, RCIA teams, deacons, college students, and inquiring lay persons who desire a basic knowledge of faith as articulated in the Apostles' Creed. It is my hope that this book will explain the meaning of the twelve articles of faith, their roots in apostolic faith, and their applicability and meaning for today.

The introduction covers background issues pertaining to the Apostles' Creed. For example, it was not actually written by the apostles but is based on the "Old Roman Creed." The Apostles' Creed was influential in Reformation debates and formed the basis of a major section of the Roman Catechism following the Council of Trent. The Apostles' Creed even forms the basis of a section the most recent *Catechism of the Catholic Church* (CCC).

Following the introduction are twelve chapters, one for each article of the Creed. Each chapter begins with the article itself, how its roots are present in Sacred Scripture (in some cases both the Old Testament and the New Testament), what the article meant for early Christians (that is, what theological truth it was conveying), how the article may have been understood later, and how the article can be understood today, looking variously at the new catechism, the *United States Catholic Catechism for Adults,* and the work of some contemporary theologians. Each chapter concludes with "The Bottom Line," summarizing the theological import of the article. Discussion questions are also provided for those who study this material in a group setting, but the questions may also be fruitful for individual reflection. The questions are designed not only as a review of the material but also as an application of its relevance and meaning for today. Though not every chapter includes each element, this is the basic structure of the book. The final chapter of the book is a conclusion.

In a book on this subject matter, recourse to the sources is sometimes required. When reference is made to Hebrew, Greek, and Latin terms, they are transliterated. The reader will notice that brackets are sometimes used in the context of quotes. The brackets are used to indicate one of two things: a) the words in brackets are not in the original quote, or b) the words in brackets are there in the language being translated. The symbol § designates an article or section in a referenced source. Further discussion of certain material or more extensive documentation of an argument can be found in the notes. Overall, however, the book is designed to be read profitably without recourse to the notes for those who might find that burdensome.

Passages from the Qur'an are taken from the A. J. Arberry translation (*The Koran Interpreted: A Translation*. Touchstone, 1996). All nonscriptural translations are my own unless otherwise indicated.

Introduction

The Apostles' Creed, with its twelve articles of faith, is familiar to many Catholics who pray the Rosary. Catholics also hear and/or recite the Apostles' Creed at children's liturgies. The creed we usually say at a regular Sunday liturgy is usually referred to as the Nicene Creed. These two creeds, the Apostles' Creed and the Nicene Creed, hold a special place in the life of the church (CCC §193). Yet neither encompasses the entirety of the Catholic faith.

It is commonly assumed that the Apostles' Creed is so named because it comes from the Twelve Apostles. Legend has it that each apostle contributed one article.[1] However, we know today that the Apostles' Creed has a much more complex history. Instead of indicating that the creed comes directly from the twelve apostles, the term *apostles' creed* is used to mean that the creed reflects what the apostles believed and taught.

The term *creed* comes from the Latin *credo* which means "I believe." (The Greek term is *symbolon*, from which we get our English word, *symbol*, which the Catechism uses with some frequency.) A creed is, then, a statement of faith. In some ways we can say Christians have had creeds from the earliest days of the church. Indeed, St. Paul seems to appeal to a creed when he says, "Jesus is Lord" (Romans 10:9). Philip baptizes the Ethiopian eunuch after he proclaims, "I believe that Jesus Christ is the Son of God" (Acts 8:37). We know that these early creeds grew in content so that it was no longer enough to claim "Jesus is Lord." Paul says in his letter to the Corinthians, "yet for us there is one God, the Father, from whom all things are and for whom we exist, and one Lord, Jesus Christ, through whom all things are and through whom we exist" (1 Corinthians 8:6). There also is the famous example of 1 Timothy 2:3-6 which seems to draw on a creedal statement to explicate the "knowledge of the truth":

> This is good and pleasing to God our savior, who wills everyone to be saved and to come to knowledge of the truth. For there is one God. There is also one mediator between God and the human race, Christ Jesus, himself human, who gave himself as ransom for all. This was the testimony at the proper time.

Early versions of creeds also grew to express other key aspects of faith in Jesus. For example, Ignatius of Antioch, who composed seven letters on his way to martyrdom in Rome (died circa 117) wrote:

> Stop your ears, therefore, when any one speaks to you at variance with Jesus Christ, who was descended from David, and was also of Mary; who was truly born, and did eat and drink. He was truly persecuted under Pontius Pilate. He was truly crucified, and (truly) died, in the sight of beings in heaven, and on earth, and under the earth. He was also truly raised from the dead, his Father quickening him, even as after the same manner his Father will so raise up us who believe in him by Christ Jesus, apart from whom we do not possess the true life.[2]

Furthermore, there was a desire not only to express faith in Jesus and the key aspects of his life and death, but there was also a need to profess a belief in God the Father and in the Spirit. For example, at the close of the Gospel of Matthew, Jesus gives his disciples a command:

"Go, therefore, and make disciples of all nations, baptizing
them in the name of the Father, and of the Son, and of the holy
Spirit, teaching them to observe all that I have commanded
you. And behold, I am with you always, until the end of the
age" (Matthew 28:19-20).

This command to baptize in the name of the Father and of the Son
and of the Holy Spirit may have given rise to the practice of professing
faith in the context of baptism. For, ultimately, a creed was professed by
catechumens immediately prior to baptism. Sometimes the catechumen
was questioned (as we do today at times in the liturgy) and in so doing
made a profession of faith in God the Father, Jesus the Son, and the Holy
Spirit. With each name, the catechumen was plunged into the waters of
baptism so that profession in the triune God was accompanied by a
triune plunge! In fact, Hippolytus, writing about A.D. 215, tells us how
baptisms were being done, and thus gives us an early form of the creed.

He who is to be baptized…is handed over by a deacon to the
presbyter who stands near the water. A presbyter holds his right
hand and makes him turn his face toward the east, near the water. Before going down into the water, his face toward the east
and standing near the water, he says this after having received
the oil of exorcism: "I believe, and submit myself to you and to
all your service, O Father, Son, and Holy Spirit."

Thus he descends into the waters; the presbyter places his hand
on his head and questions him, saying, "Do you believe in God
the Father Almighty?"

He who is baptized replies, "I believe." Then he immerses him in the water once, his hand on his head.

He questions him a second time, saying, "Do you believe in Jesus Christ, Son of God, whom the virgin Mary bore by the Holy Spirit, who came for the salvation of the human race, who was crucified in the time of Pontius Pilate, who died and was raised from the dead on the third day, ascended into heaven, is seated at the right hand of the Father, and will come to judge the living and the dead?"

He replies, "I believe." Then he immerses him in the water a second time.

He questions him a third time, saying, "Do you believe in the Holy Spirit, the Paraclete flowing from the Father and the Son?"

When he replies, "I believe," he immerses him a third time in the water. And he says each time, "I baptize you in the name of the Father, of the Son, and of the Holy Spirit, equal Trinity."[3]

As we can imagine, there were no sacramentaries in the early church. As a friend of mine likes to say, "Jesus did not hand out three-ring binders at the last supper." Different locales practiced the faith in a variety of ways, especially in the first centuries of the church. We should not be too surprised to find that while many ancient creeds were similar, it is not possible to say that all creeds were the same. Rather than one distinct formula memorized by all churches everywhere throughout the Ancient Christian Mediterranean, there were a variety of creedal statements, and most likely a variety of creeds even in the same city, perhaps even in various liturgical settings. Moreover, the creed itself, along with the Lord's Prayer, sacraments, and other cultic rituals were not to be written down on paper but on the heart.

ANCIENT FAITH FOR THE MODERN WORLD

It seems that a basic three-article formula (not unlike Matthew 28:19-20) was expanded in different ways, at different times, by a variety of communities, to express the faith of the believing community. These creedal statements were seen as legitimate expressions of faith, even though they may have differed on certain details (cf. CCC §192-193).

A variety of ancient authors give witness to the creeds that were spoken: Rufinus, Jerome, Tertullian, Justin, Irenaeus, Hippolytus, and others. These authorities might mention a particular creed and reference its locale. For example, we hear that there was a creed in Aquilea (an ancient city in Italy near modern day Venice) and a creed in Rome. The latter is known today as the "Old Roman Creed," of which the Apostles' Creed seems to have been a variant.

Old Roman Creed

The Old Roman Creed is a name used by scholars to refer to a creed, attested in many sources, that was used in Rome. Some authorities give us a Latin version. Others give us a Greek version. Scholars deduce that the Greek version is more primitive, thus pointing to its being the original language of the Old Roman Creed. Others suggest the Greek version was used for Greek-speaking catechumens and the Latin version was used for the Latin-speaking catechumens. Though we might suppose that a Roman audience would speak Latin, we also recall that Paul wrote his letter to the Romans in Greek, and the Gospel of Mark, often associated with the church at Rome, was written in Greek. For that matter, the entire New Testament was written in Greek. Since the Roman church still spoke Greek in the second century, that seems a likely date for the origin of the Old Roman Creed.

There are many witnesses to a creed in Rome. For example, the *Apostolic Traditions,* cited above, is associated with the Roman church. Tertullian (born circa A.D. 160) also tells us about a creed at Rome.

He was born a pagan in Carthage, became a Christian by 197, and was ordained a priest about 200. Sometime after 206, he seems to have become a Montanist (follower of Montanus, a mid-second-century heretic). By 213 Tertullian had completely separated from the church. He even separated from the Montanists and formed his own sect, which became known as the Tertullianists. Augustine himself later reconciled the Tertullianists with the church.

Writing as a Christian, Tertullian reflects the teaching of the church at Rome: "[The church at Rome] acknowledges one God and Lord, the creator of the universe, and Christ Jesus (born) of the virgin Mary, son of God the creator, and the resurrection of the flesh. The law and the prophets unites with the Gospels and the apostolic writings..." (*De praescriptione*, 36). While a Montanist, Tertullian wrote another work in which he makes attestation to a creed:

> The rule of faith is altogether one, alone unchangeable and irreformable: namely, of believing in one God almighty, creator of the world, and his son Jesus Christ, born of the virgin Mary, crucified under Pontius Pilate, raised on the third day from the dead, received into heaven, now seated at the right hand of the Father, to come again to judge the living, and the dead also, through the resurrection of the flesh (*De virginibus velandis*, 1.3).

Other theologians bearing witness to the Old Roman Creed include Rufinus, a contemporary of Jerome, who compares it with his own creed of Aquilea. The Old Roman Creed is also attested in Greek by Marcellus, bishop of Ancyra in Cappadocia, in an Apologia to Pope Julius I dated to 340 and preserved in Epiphanius, *Panarion*, 72.3.1. Rufinus compares the creed of his baptism at Aquilea with the creed professed at Rome. He admits that the Aquilean creed has some additions, while maintaining that the creed has apostolic origin.

So, the Old Roman Creed is attested but must be reconstructed based on scholarship, with the knowledge that some scholars may propose other, more convincing reconstructions. For example, we may compare the creed at Rome given to us by Rufinus (in Latin) with the creed at Rome given to us by Marcellus (in Greek). Beyond even the issue of language (one in Greek, the other in Latin), there are slight differences between the two creeds. Scholars then reconstruct to the best of their ability what might have been the Old Roman Creed.

Reproduced here is the creed of Rome as attested by Rufinus and reconstructed by J.N.D. Kelly. Note the differences between this creed and the Apostles' Creed we recite today.

> I believe in God the Father almighty
> And in Christ Jesus, his only Son, our Lord,
>> Who was born from the Holy Spirit and the Virgin Mary,
>> Who was crucified under Pontius Pilate and buried,
>> on the third day he rose again from the dead,
>> he ascended to heaven,
>> he sits at the Father's right hand,
>> Whence he will come to judge the living and the dead;
> And in the Holy Spirit,
>> the holy Church,
>> the remission of sins,
>> the resurrection of the flesh.[4]

Apostles' Creed

The Apostles' Creed[5] is first referred to as such in a letter from Ambrose in 389. After calling it the "Apostles' Creed," Ambrose says that "the spotless Roman church has always guarded and saved [it]" (Letter 42.5). As cited above, Rufinus was convinced of the apostolic origin of the creed and even mentioned how at the original Pentecost each apostle made a contribution to it before setting out to preach. Augustine commented on the creed in Sermon 398, also known as *On the Creed to the Catechumens.* Later in *De Symbolo*, the spurious work of a pseudo-Augustine, the writer claimed that each apostle contributed one article:

> How each apostle composed the creed.... On the tenth day after the ascension, when the disciples had gathered in fear of the Jews, the Lord sent the Spirit as he promised. It came as a glittering sword aflame. And filled with the knowledge of all languages they composed the creed.
>
> Peter said, "I believe in God, the Father almighty."
>
> Andrew said, "and in Jesus Christ his Son."
>
> James said, "Who was conceived by the Holy Spirit...born of the Virgin Mary."
>
> John said, "suffered under Pontius Pilate....was crucified, died, and was buried, according to the flesh."
>
> Thomas said, "He descended into hell...on the third day he rose from the dead."
>
> James said, "He ascended into heaven....he is seated at the right hand of God, the Father almighty."
>
> Philip said, "from there he will come to judge the living and the dead."

ANCIENT FAITH FOR THE MODERN WORLD

Bartholomew said, "I believe in the Holy Spirit."

Matthew said, "The Holy Catholic Church…the communion of saints."

Simon said, "the remission of sins."

Thaddaeus said, "the resurrection of the flesh."

Matthias said, "Life eternal" (Sermon 240, *De Symbolo* IV).

It is interesting that the list of the twelve used for the creed comes from the Gospel of Matthew ("the church's Gospel") with the name of Matthias in place of Judas, as told in Acts 1:26. Yet the list of the twelve from Acts names Jude of James as one of the twelve instead of Thaddaeus (see "Lists of the Twelve" in the appendices). The New Testament itself does not agree on the list of the twelve apostles. We are forced to follow either the Marcan/Matthean tradition or the Lucan tradition. The Gospel of John, with its fierce and overriding emphasis on Jesus, does not even bother to give us the list of the twelve.

Thus, the stage was set for the promulgation of the finalized version of the Apostles' Creed as used throughout the medieval period in the West. This "apostolic" catechetical instruction was a convenient tool for teaching the faith. The credibility of the story went unquestioned up until the fifteenth century, when an attempt at reconciliation with the Eastern Church at the Council of Florence brought the issue to the fore. The representatives of the Eastern Church doubted the authenticity and authority of the creed, as it was not in use within their church. Moreover, they argued, such a creed had its origin neither in Sacred Scripture nor in the writings of the early church fathers. Since the advent of the renaissance, most serious scholars have abandoned the idea that the creed with its twelve articles originated with the apostles. Instead, they recognize that various creeds grew along with the early church.

Martin Luther arrived on the scene in the early sixteenth century. His contribution to creedal studies was to change a single but significant word of the Apostles' Creed, that of *Catholic* to *Christian*.[6] The Roman Catholic Church responded, in a way, by making their version of the Apostles' Creed one of the bedrocks of the Roman Catechism that was produced in the wake of the Council of Trent. The Roman Catechism expressed the faith of the church around the four pillars of Creed, Ten Commandments, Lord's Prayer, and Sacraments. The *Catechism of the Catholic Church,* published in the waning years of the twentieth century, followed the Roman Catechism's four pillars.

Both the Apostles' Creed and the Nicene Creed can be found in the *Catechism of the Catholic Church.* The texts of the two creeds are reproduced between articles 184 and 185, with creeds in general being discussed from articles 185 to 197. (See pages 151-153.)

This is the Apostles' Creed as Catholics recite it today:

I believe in God,
the Father almighty,
creator of heaven and earth,
and in Jesus Christ, his only Son, our Lord.
who was conceived by the power of the Holy Spirit
born of the Virgin Mary,
suffered under Pontius Pilate,
was crucified, died, and was buried;
he descended into hell;
on the third day he rose again;
he ascended into heaven,
and is seated at the right hand of the Father;
from there he will come to judge the living and the dead.

ANCIENT FAITH FOR THE MODERN WORLD

I believe in the Holy Spirit,
the holy catholic Church,
the communion of saints,
the forgiveness of sins,
the resurrection of the body,
and life everlasting.
Amen.

In the following pages we will explore each of the articles of this creed, showing how in some cases they reflect beliefs found in the Old Testament but in many other cases they express a unique Christian perspective, especially when it comes to the person of Jesus.

Article One

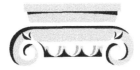

I believe in God, the Father almighty,
creator of heaven and earth.

The English phrase *I believe* is a translation of the Latin word *credo*. Each individual Christian professes a personal faith in common with the community of believers, so that the faith "I believe" is also the faith "we believe." This was how English-speaking Catholics throughout the world professed their faith in the liturgy for several decades following Vatican II. With the liturgical changes introduced during the pontificate of Benedict XVI, however, the English language translation of the creed was changed from "we believe" to "I believe," to more accurately reflect the Latin.

Moving on to the object of that belief, it is in some ways surprising that the Apostles' Creed, with its twelve articles of faith, has only one article addressing "God the Father." This is because the basic belief in God the Father is not something that has been a matter of debate or argument for Christians. It needs little clarification, and in some ways the belief in God the Father is shared with Jews, unlike the profession of faith in Jesus Christ, his Son, which is reflected in six articles or about half of the creed. Despite this seeming clarity about belief in God the Father, however, it bears mentioning the various ways in which the image of God has grown and transformed throughout the Old and New Testaments.

Old Testament

The appellations of God expressed in this article stem from the Old Testament where God is called "Father" (Psalms 68:5; 89:26; Isaiah 9:6), "almighty" (Genesis 17:1; 28:3; 35:11; 43:14; 48:3; Exodus 6:3; Psalms 68:14; 91:1; Ezekiel 10:5; Joel 1:15; Wisdom 7:25; Sirach 42:17; 50:14); and "creator of heaven and earth" (Genesis 1:1; 2:4; Isaiah 40:28; Nehemiah 9:6; Psalm 33:6-9).

The term *Father* in the Old Testament was applied to God in the sense that God was the father of Israel. For example, anthropomorphic images of God teaching Ephraim to walk convey the sense of God as parent (Hosea 11:3). In Deuteronomy 1:31, God is portrayed as carrying the Israelites through the desert as a man carries his child. The sense of God as parent is also evident in the metaphor of God hovering over his brood as an eagle would (Deuteronomy 32:10-12). God was also father to the king (2 Samuel 7:14).

Almighty is a title for God associated with the patriarchs Abraham, Isaac, and Joseph (for example, Genesis 17:1; 28:3; 35:11; 43:14; 48:3; Exodus 6:3). The Hebrew term underlying *God Almighty* is *El-Shaddai*. There were many various titles for God, such as God of the Mountain (*El-Har*); God Most High (*El-Elyon*, Genesis 14:18); God of Vision (*El-Roi*, Genesis 16:13); God Everlasting (*El-Olam*, Genesis 21:33); God of Bethel (or *El-Bethel*, or "God of the house of god," Genesis 31:13; 35:1,3,7); God the God of Israel (*El-Elohe-Israel*, Genesis 33:20); God the God of your fathers (*El-Elohe-Abikah*, Genesis 46:3); Shield (*Magen*, Genesis 15:1), and many others. Yet in the midst of all these names for God, the term *El-Shaddai*, or *God Almighty*, stands out because of its association with the patriarchs. It is an ancient title for God. In the story of God's self-revelation to Moses, God says, "I am the LORD [*YHWH*]. As God the Almighty [*El-Shaddai*] I appeared to Abraham, Isaac and Jacob, but by my name, LORD, [*YHWH*] I did not make myself known to them." (Exodus 6:2-3).

In the Exodus passage, we see that *El-Shaddai* and *YHWH* are one and the same. They are not two gods. The same God whom the patriarchs worshipped as *El-Shaddai* now calls Moses. But now, God reveals his name as YHWH. This name is also known as the "tetragrammaton" or "four-letters." This name was holy and not to be pronounced. In Greek manuscripts of the Old Testament, the four letters were often rendered as *kyrios*, or *Lord*, if they were rendered at all. In the *New American Bible*, this highly respected name for God is rendered by the all capitals, LORD. So, any time we see LORD in the *New American Bible* we recognize that the underlying Hebrew is *YHWH*. The word is written *YHWH* because biblical Hebrew script uses only consonants. One might vocalize the tetragrammaton as "Yahweh," or "Jehovah."

To be precise, the term *YHWH* does not mean *Lord* but was rendered as such to avoid saying *Yahweh*. When a Jew came across this name in the sacred text, he would not pronounce it. Instead he would say *adonai,* a Hebrew word which means "Lord." For example, in the Septuagint (the Greek translation of the Old Testament) the term *YHWH* is often rendered as *kyrios,* or *Lord*. The Greek term *kyrios* also translates the Hebrew term *adôn* (*Septuagint*, Psalm 113:7) and the Aramaic word *mare* (Theodotion's version of Daniel 2:47; 4:16,21; 5:23). Each are used in the Old Testament as a way to refer to God.[7]

The root meaning of *shaddai* is disputed. Scholars differ on its etymology. Those who translated the term into Greek or Hebrew often used *pantokrator* and/or *omnipotens*, thus indicating that the term meant for them "powerful one, strong one, or almighty." That same Greek term *pantokrator* was also used of God in the New Testament. In fact, in 2 Corinthians 6:18 Paul calls God *pantokrator* immediately after referring to God as *father* (Paul is freely quoting 2 Samuel 7:14). *Pantokrator* is also a frequent term in the book of Revelation. When St. Jerome translated the Hebrew Old Testament into Latin, he often used the term *Deus omnipotens*, or *God All-powerful/Almig*hty for *El-Shaddai*. These Greek and Latin terms are a clue that in the creed the underlying term for *pantokrator* or *omnipotens* is ultimately the Hebrew term *shaddai*. The God of the Old Testament, the God of the fathers Abraham, Isaac, and Jacob, is the same as the God of the Christians.

Another Old Testament appellation of God repeated in the Apostles' Creed is "creator of heaven and earth." This is significant in that many myths of the ancient Near East posited that the earth had been made of the dead bodies of gods, or that the sun, moon, and stars were themselves gods. Genesis 1 relates that God created the earth, the seas, the heavens, and all they contain. The sun is not a god, but is a "big light" placed in the sky by God to govern the day. The moon is not a god, but is a "little light" placed in the sky by God to govern the night. The sky itself is a firmament established by God by the voice of divine command. Creation was not difficult work for God; it was not labor intensive. Moreover, creation itself is not God. God is distinct from creation.

God is also a *good* creator. Seven times the narrator of the first creation story tells the reader that God saw that it was good. After the sixth day, creation is declared "very good." This is an important lesson for us in the modern world. The created world is good, and it is a source of goodness. Creation itself may be seen as God's first revelation. We human beings learn something of the creator by studying creation. Rather than a source of evil and temptation, creation is something good, even very good. More than that, creation is ultimately a free gift. These ideas found in the opening of the Bible may be read throughout the sacred canon and into the New Testament (Romans 1:25; 1 Peter 4:19). It comes as no surprise then to read this basic affirmation of faith in the first article of the Apostles' Creed.

New Testament

Ultimately, the earliest followers of Jesus (who were Jews) knew that they were worshipping the same God they had always worshipped, and the same God Jesus himself had worshipped. This image of God as Father was certainly apparent in the ministry of Jesus (for example, John 6:27), who taught his disciples to address God *Father, Abba* in Aramaic, translated in Greek as *Pater* (Matthew 6:9; Luke 11:2). St. Paul gives evidence that second generation Christians indeed cried "Abba" (Romans 8:15; Galatians 6:4). The father image is thus meant to convey authority as well as loving care, concern, and protection.

Thus, for the early Christians, calling God *Father* echoed the faith expressed in the Old Testament. The God of the Old Testament was the God of Jesus Christ, the God of the New Testament, the God of the Christians. This line of thinking was challenged by the second-century Christian thinker Marcion, who was later declared a heretic. He believed that the Old Testament God was so unlike the God of Jesus Christ that the Old Testament itself was inspired by the devil. Early Christians fought Marcionite thought by maintaining that both the Old Testament and the New Testament were inspired by the same God, the one God, the Father of Jesus Christ.

Despite the fact that Jesus himself, the early Christians, and centuries of Christians from then on addressed God as Father, some today find that term, or any other masculine referent for God, inadequate. Some modern theologians query whether "father language" is really appropriate when speaking of God, for God is ultimately neither male nor female.[8] These theologians claim that the father language arose in a patriarchal world that no longer corresponds to our own. The *Catechism* tells us that the Father language is used to express authority and loving care (CCC § 239). And yet, we know that mothers are able to express loving care, concern, and protection just as fathers do. In the same paragraph as that cited above, the *Catechism* says, "God's paternal tenderness can also be expressed by the image of motherhood" (CCC § 239). The *Catechism* cites two scripture passages on this: Isaiah 66:13 and Psalm 131:2. While some modern theologians are raising our awareness of the issues surrounding paternal images of God, the image of God as father remains dominant in the scriptural, liturgical, and theological tradition.

THE BOTTOM LINE

There is a God. God reveals himself as a parent to his chosen people and to all. This father image expresses the loving care and authority of God. By his love, God calls a people and makes them his own. By his authority, he creates the heavens and the earth. As creator, God is distinct from creation. God is not the same as creation but is the source of creation. Accordingly, Christians respect and care for creation but do not worship it.

DISCUSSION QUESTIONS

Refer to *Catechism of the Catholic Church*, §198-421.

- What makes the first person of the Trinity unique among the three persons to you? Explain why.

- At what times in your own prayer life do you address God as "Father?" What other names do you use to address God?

- How does your relationship with your own parent or parents inform or distract from calling God "Father"?

- How would you try to convince a non-believer that the God of the Old Testament is the same God of the New Testament?

Article Two

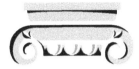

I believe in Jesus Christ
his only Son, our Lord.

The second article of the Apostles' Creed begins with the Latin verb *credo*, or *I believe*, signaling that this is now a new topic, as it were. We are no longer talking about God the Father; we are now proclaiming our belief in "Jesus," the second person of the Trinity (though the term *Trinity* is not used in the creed). We will see that most of the articles in the creed have to do with Jesus, because the issues at stake during the formulation of the creed were primarily Christological. That is, the theological debates centered on the person of Jesus, his identity, and what God has done through him for humanity. So, we are not surprised to find half of the articles in the creed about Jesus, and only one about God the Father and one about the Holy Spirit.

Jesus

The name *Jesus* sets the person in a historical context. The Greek name *Iēsous* is derived from the Hebrew name *Yēshû*, a shortened form of the Hebrew name *Yeshûa* (Ezra 2:2; Nehemiah 3:19), which itself is a contraction of *Yĕhôshuā* (Joshua 1:1), meaning "Yahweh, help!" These Hebrew names were common.[9] In some ways we can say it is equivalent to the name *Josh* as a shortened form of *Joshua*.[10] This name was common in the first century, almost like *Bob* or *John* today.

Christ

In the creed, as in much of the New Testament, the word *Christ* is used almost as a last name of Jesus. Indeed, one grade-schooler told me that Jesus Christ was the son of Mary and Joseph Christ. But of course, *Christ* is not the last name of Jesus. It is instead a title based on the Greek term *Christos*, which is itself a translation of the Hebrew term *mashîā*, or *Messiah*. The term means "anointed" and was used in a variety of ways in the Old Testament, including to refer to historical kings of Israel (for example, 1 Samuel 16:6) like David in particular (for example, 2 Samuel

1:14), and even the pagan king Cyrus (Isaiah 45:1). At times it is used as an adjective for a high priest (for example, Leviticus 4:5).[11] So today, when we call Jesus the Christ, we are saying that he is the Messiah, God's anointed.

Messiah, or *Christ*, is one of the earliest titles for Jesus. Paul, in his letter to the Romans, specifically referred to Jesus as the Messiah (Romans 9:5), and throughout the letters he used *Christ* as something of a second name for Jesus.

It is important to recall that Jesus did not fulfill the role of Messiah in the way expected by first-century Jews. That is, many first-century Jews expected a Davidic King who would restore the independence of Israel, casting off Roman occupation and thereby bringing peace and prosperity to the people. Certainly today, Jews do not believe Jesus is, or was, the Messiah. Though "Messianic Jews" exist, because of their belief in Jesus as the Christ, they are not considered Jews by most Jews. Neither, too, are they considered Christians by most Christians, since they do not accept the divinity of Christ.

Once at a college campus interreligious dialogue, a freshman asked the rabbi a question that perhaps only a bold freshman can ask. "Why don't you Jews just accept the fact that Jesus is the Messiah?" The rabbi, however, did not shy away from answering it: "Jews do not accept Jesus as the Messiah because he does not fulfill the job description. The Old Testament says nothing about a suffering Messiah. The Messiah who is expected is a Davidic King who will reign in Israel, establishing peace and prosperity. Jesus did not do that, so he is not the Messiah." He went further in saying that an argument could be made that, since the time of Jesus, Jews have experienced anything but peace and often this has been at the hands of Christians.

The rabbi's response is certainly correct from a strictly Jewish perspective. Christians believe Jesus fulfills what it means to be Messiah in

ANCIENT FAITH FOR THE MODERN WORLD

a way that was completely unforeseen. Indeed the church states as much when it says in the 2002 Pontifical Biblical Commission document, *The Jewish People and their Sacred Scripture in the Christian Bible:*

> Christian faith recognizes the fulfilment, in Christ, of the Scriptures and the hopes of Israel, but it does not understand this fulfilment as a literal one. Such a conception would be reductionist. In reality, in the mystery of Christ crucified and risen, fulfilment is brought about in a manner unforeseen. It includes transcendence. Jesus is not confined to playing an already fixed role — that of Messiah — but he confers, on the notions of Messiah and salvation, a fullness which could not have been imagined in advance; he fills them with a new reality; one can even speak in this connection of a "new creation." It would be wrong to consider the prophecies of the Old Testament as some kind of photographic anticipations of future events. All the texts, including those which later were read as messianic prophecies, already had an immediate import and meaning for their contemporaries before attaining a fuller meaning for future hearers. The messiahship of Jesus has a meaning that is new and original.[12]

So, only in faith can we say that Jesus is the Messiah, that Jesus is the Christ. That is to say, rather than a philosophical statement or one deduced from strict logic, the claim that Jesus is the Messiah is one that can be made only by faith. He is King in the sense that he is establishing the Kingdom of God, with radically different values than the kingdom of this world.

Son of God

This article of the creed also mentions that Jesus is the only son of God. In this, the creed is echoing language from the Gospel of John wherein the prologue states "only begotten of God" (John 1:18).While it is true that Paul (Romans 8:15; Galatians 4:6) and others claim that Jesus gives us the power to call God *Father*, and therefore we are sons and daughters of God, Jesus is God's son in a unique way. We recall that at Jesus' baptism he is called God's son (Mark 1:11). Mark also tells us that Jesus cried *"Abba"* (the Aramaic term for *Father*) in the garden of Gethsemane (Mark 14:36). Jesus, as the unique son of God (John 1:18), gives others the power to call God *Father*. The most famous example would be the "Lord's Prayer," or the "Our Father" (Matthew 6:9-13). When Jesus called God *Father* and said "the Father and I are one" (John 10:30), his enemies understood this as blasphemy, for he was making himself equal with God (John 5:18).

Lord

Finally, this article concludes with the term, our *Lord*. With this appellation, we come to what scholastic theologians termed *Christus pro nobis*, or *Christ for us*. After we make claims about who Jesus is, the next natural question is: What does Jesus mean to us? What is the salvific import of these Christological claims? For the Christian, Jesus is "our Lord."

So, when the early Christians began to call Jesus *kyrios*, or Lord, they were expressing something significant, exalting Jesus to the status of YHWH. Perhaps nowhere is that more evident than in the hymn that Paul quotes to the Philippians which concludes: "every knee should bend, of those in heaven and on earth and under the earth, and every tongue confess that Jesus Christ is Lord, to the glory of God the Father." Though Paul himself sometimes uses *kyrios* for Yahweh (for example, 1

Thessalonians 4:6), he also applies the same title to Jesus. Paul's hymn also conveys a larger point, however, which is that though Jesus is on par with Yahweh, he is not to be identified with him (cf. Philippians 2:11). There is both identity and distinction. This kind of expression will set the stage for the later Christological and Trinitarian debates of the third and fourth centuries.

Even pagan sources tell us that the early Christians sang hymns to Christ as though he were God. For example, Pliny (circa 63-113), the governor of Asia, had arrested some Christians. After he had them tortured, they confessed among other things that "on a set day they used to meet before dawn and sing a hymn among themselves to Christ, as though he were a god."[13]

The term *Lord* is also significant in the Gospel of John. For example, John opens his gospel with the famous prologue, "In the beginning was the Word, and the Word was with God, and the Word was God" (John 1:1). The prologue continues by expressing incarnational language, "And the Word became flesh and made his dwelling among us" (John 1:14a). Jesus is the Word of God made flesh, who lived among us. Not until after the death and resurrection of Jesus, does a human being (Thomas) proclaim, "My Lord and my God!" to which Jesus responds, "Have you come to believe because you have seen me? Blessed are those who have not seen and have believed." The gospel then concludes: "Now Jesus did many other signs in the presence of (his) disciples that are not written in this book. But these are written that you may (come to) believe that Jesus is the Messiah, the Son of God, and that through this belief you may have life in his name" (John 20:28-30).[14]

Thus, the term *Lord* in the Old Testament and in the New Testament has profound meaning. It was used in the Old Testament to refer to YHWH, and in the New Testament to express Jesus' identity for

Christians. Jesus is on par with YHWH such that true faith in him leads to an expression of him as "my Lord and my God." This article in the creed echoes the early Christian belief that Jesus Christ is our Lord.

THE BOTTOM LINE

Jesus was a historical figure who lived in Galilee in the early first century A.D. He was hailed as *Christ*, which means "Messiah," or "anointed one," to designate that he was God's anointed. His relationship with God is so unique that he can be called God's only son (John 1:18). With respect to humanity, he is our Lord, on par with YHWH.

DISCUSSION QUESTIONS

Refer to *Catechism of the Catholic Church*, §422-455.

- What do the titles *Messiah* and *Lord* mean to you? Is there a title you prefer to use for Jesus instead of *Messiah* or *Lord*? If so, what and why?

- What does it mean to you that Jesus is the son of God?

- What does it mean for us to be children of God?

- How would you explain to a non-Christian what we believe in calling Jesus *the Christ*?

Article Three

He was conceived
by the power of the Holy Spirit
and born of the Virgin Mary.

The third article of the Apostles' Creed sets the stage for many of the Christological debates that eventually culminated in the language of the *Catechism*: "Jesus Christ is true God and true man" (CCC § 464). To say that Jesus was conceived by the power of the Holy Spirit echoes the language of the Gospels of Matthew and Luke, which comprise the only New Testament accounts of the birth of Jesus.

Born of the Virgin Mary

Though there is New Testament evidence that Mary is the mother of Jesus (Matthew 1:16; Mark 6:3; Luke 1:27-38; Acts 1:14), neither Mark nor John mentions the virginal birth. The Gospel of John does not even give us Mary's name.[15] Matthew and Luke are left to tell the story of the virgin birth.

At the conclusion of the genealogy of the Messiah, after going such lengths to indicate paternity from one generation to the next, Matthew lists "Jacob the father of Joseph, the husband of Mary. Of her was born Jesus who is called the Messiah" (Matthew 1:16). He thus makes clear that Jesus was born of Mary. Rather than being named as the father of Jesus, or purported father of Jesus, Joseph is referred to merely as the husband of Mary. At the same time, Matthew also states clearly that Jesus was conceived by the Holy Spirit so that he will be called *Emmanuel* which means "God is with us" (Matthew 1:23). Matthew sees in the virgin birth a fulfillment of the prophecy in Isaiah. As Matthew recalls:

> …behold, the angel of the Lord appeared to him in a dream
> and said, "Joseph, son of David, do not be afraid to take Mary
> your wife into your home. For it is through the holy Spirit that
> this child has been conceived in her. She will bear a son and
> you are to name him Jesus, because he will save his people from
> their sins."

All this took place to fulfill what the Lord had said through the prophet: "Behold, the virgin shall be with child and bear a son, and they shall name him Emmanuel," which means "God is with us." (Matthew 1:20-23).

It should be noted that in Isaiah the Hebrew text actually says, "Therefore the Lord himself will give you a sign: the young woman, pregnant and about to bear a son, shall name him Emmanuel" (Isaiah 7:14). Notice that the key term *young woman* from Isaiah has become *virgin* in Matthew's gospel. Why the difference? The Hebrew term *almah* means "young woman," without respect to virginity. When the Hebrew was translated into Greek in about the second century B.C., the Greek translators used the term *parthenos* to translate the Hebrew *almah*. The Greek term *parthenos* does mean *unmarried girl*, or *virgin*. Matthew, writing in Greek, was using the Greek version of what we call the Old Testament. So, he interpreted a virgin birth as the fulfillment of Scripture.

This gospel passage is significant because here Matthew is telling us that God was instrumental in the birth of Jesus. Recall that Matthew refers to Joseph not as the father of Jesus but as the husband of Mary. Even in Mark 6:3, Jesus is referred to as "son of Mary." Not naming the father would have been uncommon and is a clue to questionable circumstances regarding Jesus' paternity. It seems something unusual happened with the birth of Jesus. Matthew goes further in that he lists the generations from Abraham to include four women who also gave birth under difficult or abnormal circumstances: Tamar (1:3), Rahab (1:5a), Ruth (1:5b), and the wife of Uriah (1:6).

The story of Tamar is told in Genesis 38. She played the harlot and conceived the twins Perez and Zerah by her father-in-law Judah. Rahab (Joshua 2:1) was a harlot too. Living in Jericho, she helped the spies of

Joshua and was therefore spared when that city was destroyed. Ruth was not an Israelite, but a Moabite who married into the people of Israel (Book of Ruth). The wife of Uriah's actual name is Bathsheba. Matthew seems to employ verbal gymnastics to avoid even saying her name. King David seduced Bathsheba and had her husband Uriah killed in battle (2 Samuel 11-12). She later became the mother of Solomon, who would succeed David as king. Why does Matthew mention these four women? Perhaps he is reminding us that the Davidic line has been peppered with unusual and somewhat questionable circumstances. Abnormalities are not abnormal with God. Jesus, known as Son of Mary, was conceived while Mary was a virgin. A virgin birth in fact fulfills scripture.

In Luke, the angel Gabriel announces to the Virgin Mary that she is to bear a son. Mary asks, "How can this be?" With our knowledge of biology, some contemporary thinkers have asked the same. How was Mary's egg fertilized? In essence, that modern question is simply a more precise way of asking Mary's question, "How can this be?" The angel does not go into a detailed discussion on pregnancy in the ancient world. Instead, the angel tells Mary that the power of the Most High will overshadow her. This is Luke's way of saying what Matthew also says: Jesus is son of God *and* son of Mary.

Both Luke and Matthew make it clear that Mary was a virgin when she conceived and gave birth to Jesus. Later tradition goes further in stating that Mary was "ever-virgin," though it should be recognized that neither the New Testament nor the creed itself says this. However, each Sunday millions of Catholics today pray in the penitential rite of the Mass, the Confiteor:

> I confess to almighty God,
>   and to you, my brothers and sisters,
>   that I have greatly sinned

in my thoughts and in my words,
in what I have done and in what I have failed to do,
through my fault, through my fault,
through my most grievous fault;
therefore I ask blessed Mary ever-Virgin,
all the Angels and Saints,
and you, my brothers and sisters,
to pray for me to the Lord our God.

The Confiteor is much later than the Apostles' Creed. The version above is that which Catholics have prayed since Pope Benedict's new translation of the Roman Missal in 2011. The translation of the Latin is more literal than that used from post-Vatican II to 2011. The particular words that concern us here, *blessed Mary ever-Virgin*, are a direct translation of *beatam Mariam semper Vírginem* and have been in use in various, though not all, versions of the Confiteor since the Middle Ages. But the reference to the "ever-Virgin" Mary, or her perpetual virginity, is a theological idea whose origins go back to Epiphanius and Jerome. Both the New Testament and the Apostles' Creed suffice it to say that Mary was a virgin when she gave birth (Matthew 1:25).

Jesus: Human and Divine

Before the gospels were composed, Paul wrote letters. In Romans, his most famous letter, Paul employs a creedal fragment in a rhetorical flourish about God's Son. A credal fragment is a phrase or quotation that is already known in its set form to the author and/or his or her readers. It is referred to as a fragment because it is not a complete sentence. In the particular case of Romans, scholars generally agree that the fragment is the section in italics below:

Paul, a slave of Christ Jesus, called to be an apostle and set apart for the gospel of God, which he promised previously through his prophets in the holy scriptures, the gospel about his Son, *descended from David according to the flesh, but established as Son of God in power according to the spirit of holiness through resurrection from the dead,* Jesus Christ our Lord (Romans 1:1-4).

We can see the parallel structure of this early creedal fragment more clearly if we display it as such:

descended from David	according to the flesh, but
established as Son of God in power	according to the spirit of holiness through resurrection from the dead

This outline attempts to show that "descended from David" is parallel to "established as Son of God in power." Likewise, "according to the flesh" is parallel to "according to the spirit of holiness." That "spirit of holiness" is due to "the resurrection from the dead." Thus, the creedal fragment expresses a fundamental belief about Jesus. That is, he is descended from David according to the flesh (human), and he was declared to be Son of God by resurrection from the dead (divine). Thus, the creedal fragment expresses in a seminal way what later generations will refer to as both the humanity and the divinity of Jesus.

The Apostolic Fathers also wrestled with this mystery. For example, Ignatius of Antioch (died 107), wrote:

There is only one physician, who is both flesh and spirit, born and unborn, God in man, true life in death, both from Mary and from God, first subject to suffering and then beyond it, Jesus Christ our Lord.[16]

Commentators on Ignatius have recognized that "when Ignatius refers to Christ as 'both fleshly and spiritual' (Ephesians 7.2; cf. Smyrnaeans 3.3), he has in mind the union of the divine and human in the God-Man and thus anticipates the classical two-nature Christology."[17]

This divine-human balance, however, has historically been difficult for Christians to strike. Many people today, for example, seem to be hidden docetists. Docetism was an early heresy that stressed the divinity of Jesus to the detriment of his humanity. Today many Christians may sympathize with this heresy in believing Jesus was fully divine but not really accepting that he was fully human. Even though we say the words (in the Nicene Creed) *fully divine and fully human*, it is difficult to unpack their meaning and appropriate application. For example, since Jesus was fully human, he had to grow in wisdom and knowledge (Luke 2:40). That means, among other things, that he learned how to speak. He learned how to read. He made mistakes and learned from his mistakes. Yet he did not sin (Hebrews 4:15). Sometimes modern Christians have the idea that Jesus was almost a divine actor on the stage, fully aware of everything around him so that he did not have to learn anything. However, if this were the case, Jesus would not have been fully human, for that is not the way human beings are.

On the other hand, there are some Christians who stress the humanity of Jesus to such an extent that they seem to deny or delay Jesus' divinity. For example, adoptianists (from the Latin term *adoptiani*) claimed that Jesus was a human being who was adopted by God because of his good deeds and merits. Perhaps one of the most famous protagonists from this camp would be Thomas Jefferson, a founding father of the United States rather than scholar of the Bible. His book, *The Life and Morals of Jesus of Nazareth*, condensed the life of Jesus to that of his ethical teachings, removing all traces of the miracles or anything supernatural, including the resurrection. For Jefferson, Jesus becomes

ANCIENT FAITH FOR THE MODERN WORLD

an ethical teacher, hardly divine.

In the Apostles' Creed, the article stating that Jesus was conceived by the power of the Holy Spirit expresses his filial relationship with God, his divinity. Jesus incarnated God. Jesus fully expressed the love of God in the world in a way that nobody else could, for he and the Father are one. To say that he was born of Mary expresses his humanity. Jesus incarnated humanity and fully expressed what it means to be human. He was one with humanity.

Later councils reflecting later debates by church fathers continue to tease out the meaning and precise definition of this "human and divine" relationship. For example, the fifth century Council of Chalcedon reaches a climax of Christological language when the church declares that Jesus is a divine person who has a human and divine nature. But it can be a challenge to translate that precise fifth-century definition with roots in the philosophy of that age, to the twenty-first century when *person,* and even *nature,* means something different. It is true that we can speak in good, clear Chalcedonian terms and say that Jesus is a divine person, not a human person. But to say in the twenty-first century to a twenty-first century audience that Jesus is not a human person would in effect deny the mystery of the incarnation, as we use the term *person* differently in common language than they did in the Chalcedonian debate.

Still, some modern catechists and religious educators go to great lengths to teach that Jesus was a divine person with a human and divine nature. As we have seen, that is good Chalcedonian language, but it is centuries removed from the New Testament and more than a millennium removed from our time. It might not be a surprise that it can be difficult for catechists to lay the groundwork of fifth-century philosophy before teaching who Christ is and how he was defined for that age. In fact, simply stating that Jesus is not a human person but a divine person may actually do more to obfuscate our faith than to elucidate it.

Our faith should be more than simply parroting old creedal formulas that were written in a different language, at a different time, and to an audience that held different philosophical presuppositions. Instead, it is our task to understand and contemplate something of the mysteries the creeds were trying to encapsulate. This task is more difficult, but it is ultimately more rewarding.

Of course, Jesus' divinity and humanity is one of the central mysteries of Christian faith. *Mystery* in this sense does not mean, "Nobody will ever fully understand this so I won't think about it." *Mystery* instead means that no matter how fully we plumb the depths, there is always more to learn, more to ponder. Thus we say that the universe is a mystery. The more we understand about the universe, the more we see how much there is to know. It seems we will never exhaust the mysteries of the universe. That does not mean that we do not think about the mysteries of the universe. Quite the contrary, we think about its mysteries and ponder them often. So it is with the person of Christ. We will not exhaust the mystery of the humanity and divinity of Jesus; rather, the mystery of Christ's humanity and divinity will exhaust us. We will continue to approach it anew, learn more about it, plumb its depths. The fundamental mystery of the person of Jesus and his divine and human nature are expressed in this one article of faith.

Thus, this article reflects New Testament faith, as expressed particularly in Matthew, Luke, John, and Paul, and it will be developed in later councils and creeds.

THE BOTTOM LINE

Jesus' unique relationship with God is expressed by Matthew and Luke in the story of his conception. Jesus was not conceived by normal marital relations. Rather, he was conceived by the power of the Holy Spirit, the dynamic presence of God in the world. At the same time, Jesus was born in the natural way of a woman, a virgin named Mary. Her virginity at the time of his birth gives testimony to his conception by the Holy Spirit. John says Jesus was the only-begotten of God, without any reference to a virginal birth. Paul lays the foundation for later Christological debates by expressing in a seminal way both the humanity and divinity of Jesus.

DISCUSSION QUESTIONS

Refer to *Catechism of the Catholic Church*, §456-570.

- What does it mean to you that Jesus is divine? What does it mean for us that Jesus is human?

- What are the times in your spiritual life when you tend to focus on Jesus' humanity? What are the times in your spiritual life when you tend to focus on Jesus' divinity? Give examples of each.

- What scripture passages might you cite to demonstrate that Jesus was fully human? What scripture passages might you cite to demonstrate that Jesus was fully divine?

Article Four

He suffered under Pontius Pilate,
was crucified, died, and was buried.

This article of the Apostles' Creed situates the person of Jesus in history by moving from the conception and birth of Jesus to his suffering and death under a particular Roman prefect. There is no mention of Jesus' earthly ministry, his teaching, healing, or prophetic acts. Instead, we move immediately to the Paschal mystery, the suffering, death, burial, and ultimate resurrection of Christ.

Jesus suffered

The article clearly states that Jesus suffered. The Greek verb *to suffer* is *paschein*. The Latin noun form is *passio*, from which the English term *passion* is derived. So the suffering of Jesus is his passion. The fact that Jesus suffered is present in the New Testament in the Synoptic Gospels (Matthew 17:12; Mark 8:31; Luke 22:15) and in Hebrews 2:18; 5:8; 2 Corinthians 1:5; and many other passages. The suffering, death, and crucifixion of Jesus were undeniable and had to be explained theologically by the early Christians.

For these early Christians, the suffering servant songs of Isaiah (42:1-4; 49:1-7; 50:4-11; 52:13-53:12) became one interpretive key for understanding the suffering of Jesus. One passage in Isaiah in particular claims that God uses the suffering of his servant to justify (that is, to put in a right relationship with God) the many (Isaiah 53:11-12). This certainly seems to be the way 1 Peter understands it, for 1 Peter 2:22 quotes Isaiah 53:9 explicitly before alluding to other Isaiah passages in the following verses (1 Peter 2:23-25). 1 Peter 2:21 states clearly that "Christ also suffered for you," and says again in 1 Peter 3:18 that "Christ also suffered for sins."

The fact that Jesus suffered is certainly an article of faith, as we see from the Apostles' Creed. Still, it is possible to proclaim the message of Jesus without an over-emphasis on suffering. For example, the term *suffering* never appears in the Gospel of John with respect to Jesus or anyone else. There is not even an "agony" in the garden. Instead, the garden is the scene for the prayer of Jesus for the unity of his disciples, the coming of the Spirit, the teaching on the vine and branches, and other vignettes. In the Gospel of John, Jesus is crucified but it is more akin to being raised in glory than suffering (John 3:14; 12:32; 21:19). This reminds us that although Jesus' suffering is an article of faith, Christianity can also emphasize Christ's glory vis-à-vis the suffering.

Therefore, New Testament authors generally explained the suffering of Jesus in theological terms: that Christ's suffering was vicarious, that is, for others. Isaiah 53 provided a precise interpretive lens for this approach. Other New Testament authors, such as John, chose not to emphasize the suffering at all. Instead, in the Gospel of John, the cross is Jesus' place of glory.

Pontius Pilate

Jesus suffered at the hands of the Roman authority Pontius Pilate, as each of the gospels, the Acts of the Apostles, and even 1 Timothy 6:13 indicate. There is extra-biblical evidence that shows Pilate was the prefect (governor) of Judea from A.D. 26-36.[18] Judea was an imperial province rather than a senatorial province. Thus, the prefect was the vicar (that is, official representative) of the emperor, with full executive and judicial powers. That is, he enforced Roman law and acted as judge in the province.

As an occupying power, the Romans reserved the right to administer capital punishment to themselves. Aside from being standard Roman practice attested to by Latin authors, we see evidence of this in Scripture (John 8:31) and in extra-biblical literature such as Josephus' *Jewish Wars* (2.8.1). This fact is significant for the dating of Stephen's martyrdom (Acts 7:54-60). Acts tells us that Stephen was stoned by the high priest and council. We may surmise that it was only in the absence of a Roman prefect (during the time between Pilate's departure in A.D. 36 and the naming of the next prefect, Marcellus)[19] that the council would feel bold enough to exact capital punishment without Roman approval.

Though some New Testament texts portray Pilate as hesitant in ordering the execution of Jesus, other historical texts show us that Pilate did not hesitate to execute hundreds of people at a time (Josephus, *Jewish Antiquities,* 18.3.2; 18.4.1). Indeed it was because of Pilate's ruthlessness that he was eventually recalled to Rome in A.D. 36.[20]

Why do some New Testament authors portray Pilate as hesitant? For example, Mark claims that the Sanhedrin were guilty of having condemned Jesus (10:33; 14:64), even though it was Pilate who handed him over to death (15:15) after finding no reason to accuse him (15:14). Moreover, Matthew says that Pilate was reluctant to take responsibility for Jesus' death (27:24), to which "all the people" responded, "his blood be on us and on our children" (27:25). It seems that the New Testament authors were attempting to affix blame for Jesus' death on the Jews rather than on the Romans, who had the power to execute. Of course, by the time Luke, Matthew, and John were writing, and perhaps even as early as Mark, the city of Jerusalem and the Jerusalem temple had already been destroyed by the Romans. As the Catholic Church teaches:

> ...the Gospel of Matthew reflects a situation of tension and even opposition between the two communities [Christians and Jews]. In it Jesus foresees that his disciples will be flogged in the synagogues and pursued from town to town (23:34). Matthew therefore is concerned to provide for the Christians' defense. Since that situation has radically changed, Matthew's polemic need no longer interfere with relations between Christians and Jews, and the aspect of continuity can and ought to prevail. It is equally

necessary to say this in relation to the destruction of the city and the Temple. This downfall is an event of the past which henceforth ought to evoke only deep compassion.[21]

Thus, the gospel writers, coming from their perspective vis-à-vis some Jews of their day, were (among other things) explaining in a theological way the destruction of the Temple, the mission to the Gentiles, and the resistance that many Jews had to the Christian message. Thus, in the passion narratives it was convenient to affix blame on the Jewish leaders, the Sanhedrin, and the crowds, rather than on Pilate himself who ultimately held the power to inflict capital punishment. Indeed, even as Mark tells it, the fact that Pilate recognized Jesus as innocent but allowed him to be crucified does not speak well either for Roman justice or for Pilate's character.

Crucifixion

Jesus not only suffered at the hands of Pilate but was crucified. The term *crucify* literally means "to make a cross." This form of capital punishment originated in Persia and was perfected by the Romans. It was a rather common form of public execution.

One of the most famous examples of crucifixion might be Spartacus and the slave rebellion in the first century B.C. Spartacus led a rebellion of slaves over 120,000 strong. An ancient Roman author tells us that when the Romans finally put down the rebellion, they crucified 6,000 survivors along the Via Appia, the road that runs from Rome to Capua.[22] Incidentally, according to Acts 28:13-16, this is the same road that Paul took into Rome. The 1960 Stanley Kubrick film *Spartacus* starring Kirk Douglas, Laurence Olivier, and Jean Simmons, depicts the crucifixion of Spartacus and the other rebellious slaves along the Via Appia.

Crucifixion was not simply public execution but public humilia-

ANCIENT FAITH FOR THE MODERN WORLD

tion, since the person was left to hang (usually naked) until death by asphyxiation, thirst, or exposure to the elements.

Christians today usually do not reflect on the humiliation that accompanied this form of execution, focusing instead on the suffering, or how much it hurt. Yet the humility and humiliation of Jesus was part of the early Christian message (Philippians 2:7-8; cf. Acts 8:33).

The humiliation entailed in death by crucifixion was compounded by the setting in which the punishment took place. As we know from the Gospel of John, Jesus' followers had hailed him as the Messiah, "king of Israel," as he entered Jerusalem (John 12:13). By placing the sign "Jesus of Nazareth, King of the Jews" over the cross, the instrument of Jesus' crucifixion, it was as though the Romans were mocking not only Jesus but those who had hailed his entry into Jerusalem.

Other aspects of Jesus' execution were equally offensive. For example, in the book of Deuteronomy we find this intriguing passage:

> If a man guilty of a capital offense is put to death and his corpse hung on a tree, it shall not remain on the tree overnight. You shall bury it the same day; otherwise, since God's curse rests on him who hangs on a tree, you will defile the land which the LORD, your God, is giving you as an inheritance (Deuteronomy 21:22-23).

Thus we see that according to the book of Deuteronomy, a crucified person (for this is how the passage was understood in the first century A.D.) was thereby considered cursed by God. What better way for the authorities to demonstrate that Jesus is *not* the messiah but to crucify him, that is, hang him from a tree and thus show that he is cursed by God? A cursed messiah is a contradiction and thus, for followers of Jesus at least, his crucifixion becomes a theological dilemma. How can this person be the Messiah? The Messiah is to be king of Israel, restoring independence to the land as did King David. The Messiah is not to be crucified, much less suffer. In fact, nowhere in the Old Testament does it state that the Messiah will suffer. Isaiah speaks of a suffering servant, but not a suffering Messiah.[23] Paul knew well the theological quandary he faced:

> For Jews demand signs and Greeks look for wisdom, but we proclaim Christ crucified, a stumbling block to Jews and foolishness to Gentiles, but to those who are called, Jews and Greeks alike, Christ the power of God and the wisdom of God. For the foolishness of God is wiser than human wisdom, and the weakness of God is stronger than human strength (1 Corinthians 1:22-25).

We now hear Paul in a new light when he says that we preach Christ (the Messiah) crucified, a stumbling block to Jews and folly to the Greeks. Why is this a stumbling block? Precisely because *crucifixion* means "cursed by God," and *Messiah* means "anointed by God." It is a stumbling block because a crucified Messiah goes against the plain sense of scripture (Mosaic Law). The Greeks consider this folly. Paul for his part recognizes in this crucified Messiah the plan of God. God's wisdom looks foolish. God's power looks weak.

Paul also wrestles with Deuteronomy 21:13 in his letter to the Galatians. Paul believes that the law places humanity under a curse. Yet Christ dying the way he did (by crucifixion), became accursed and thereby took upon himself the curse of the law. When he died, so did the law. Now, by means of his death and resurrection, a right relationship with God is based not on external observance of Mosaic Law but on life in the Spirit that flows from faith in Jesus Christ. A right relationship with God is no longer limited to Jews but is now extended to all humanity, to Jew and Greek alike (cf. Galatians 3:13-14).

Paul thus truly grappled with this mystery of faith: a crucified Messiah. At times we may simply express faith in Jesus Christ crucified, without appreciating how incompatible this is with a plain reading of the Old Testament. Our faith is built on the faith of the apostles. Paul, for one, did much to demonstrate that a crucified Messiah actually expresses God's power and wisdom.

Jesus died

In the creed, we recite that Jesus is the Messiah; he suffered; he was crucified; and he died. It is significant that the creed states that Jesus died. There were early schisms based on this point alone. Some could admit that Jesus was crucified, but they would not claim that he died. Indeed, this is one point over which Muslims and Christians disagree today. The Qur'an states:

> And for their saying, "We slew the Messiah, Jesus son of Mary, the Messenger of God" — yet they did not slay him, neither crucified him, only a likeness of that was shown to them. Those who are at variance concerning him surely are in doubt regarding him; they have no knowledge of him, except the following of surmise; and they slew him not of a certainty — no indeed. God raised him up to Him; God is All-mighty, All-wise (4.157).

For Christians, the burial confirms the death. That is, we don't bury people who are alive. We bury the dead. To say that Jesus was buried is akin to underlining the fact that he died.

This article of faith reflects the even more ancient articulation by Paul in the fifteenth chapter of 1 Corinthians, wherein he recalls what was handed on to him:

For I handed on to you as of first importance what I also received: that Christ died for our sins in accordance with the scriptures; that he was buried; that he was raised on the third day in accordance with the scriptures; that he appeared to Cephas, then to the Twelve (1 Corinthians 15:3-5).

If we arrange this early Christian creed according to its four "that" statements we can see clearly that the second and the fourth statements confirm the first and the third respectively.

1. that Christ died for our sins in accordance with the scriptures;
2. that he was buried;
3. that he was raised on the third day in accordance with the scriptures;
4. that he appeared to Cephas, then to the Twelve.

The burial confirms the death. That is, the statement that Christ was buried substantiates the claim that he died, much like the statement that he appeared to Cephas substantiates the claim that he was raised. Scholars generally agree that Paul wrote 1 Corinthians about A.D. 57. He preached to the Corinthians, in Corinth, about AD 51-52. It would have been at that time that he gave them this formula that he himself was given. When would he have received this? According to his own words, he was in Jerusalem only twice before: once for fifteen days (circa A.D. 36) and once more to attend the "Jerusalem Council" (circa A.D. 50).[24] Perhaps he learned this early creed from the Jerusalem church at one of these visits. At any rate, the formula itself can be no later than A.D. 50, at most some twenty years after the death and resurrection of Jesus.

Ever since the death of Jesus, theologians and other Christians have been wrestling with that fact and with how to think about it theologically. Did Jesus *have to* die? Why was he crucified? Was this part of a grand plan, or is it simply how human beings reacted to Jesus? Various answers throughout history have focused primarily on the theory of atonement. That is, Jesus' death brought humanity to God according to a foreordained plan. In some way, Jesus' death appeased God or God demanded the blood-sacrifice of his Son. While some of these theological ideas may stem from certain New Testament authors, contemporary theologians are questioning whether such ideas are relevant to a twenty-first-century audience. Does God truly demand the blood-sacrifice of his Son? Is there really a divine plan that foresees each and every event? Are we all merely actors on a divine stage? Certainly many atheists are reacting to precisely this notion of God. For example, Susan Jacoby wrote recently on the WashingtonPost.com weblog, *On Faith* that:

> If there were a deity responsible for both human evil and impersonal natural disasters, I would hate him. I would prefer to go to hell rather than to make bargains with such a cruel, capricious Master of the Universe.[25]

Rather than propose a God who is pleased with blood-sacrifice or who interferes to stop some cases of moral evil and natural disaster but not others, a different way of theologizing about Christ's death may be this: Christ is the enfleshment, the embodiment of God's love in the world. What is the human response to incarnate divine love? Our response is misunderstanding, anger, hostility, and violence to the point of murder. Ultimately, we kill it.

Despite our actions, however, God has an altogether different response, which is to raise Jesus from the dead. God has the final word. Our cruel inhumanity to one another, our cruel inhumanity even to incarnate love, will be overcome by the love of God, who raises even the dead to new life. Christian theologians will continue to plumb the depths of the death and resurrection of Jesus for meaning. This is not something we exhaust. The mystery of incarnate love exhausts us.

THE BOTTOM LINE
Pontius Pilate was a historical figure who was the Roman governor of Judea, with a reputation for ruthlessness. He was the authority under whom Jesus suffered, was crucified, and died. Jesus, then, suffered capital punishment at the hands of the state. He truly died and was buried. In so doing, Jesus did not explain away suffering and death, but he did give meaning to it.

DISCUSSION QUESTIONS
Refer to *Catechism of the Catholic Church,* §571-630.

- What do you think is the proper relationship between faith and the governing power? Explain

- Where do you stand on the issue of capital punishment? Does the fact that Jesus died at the hands of the state make any difference as to where you stand on that issue?

- Was it necessary that Jesus suffer? Why? What meaning does Jesus give to suffering?

- How would Christian faith be different if we claimed that Jesus did not truly die?

Article Five

He descended into hell.
On the third day he rose again.

This fifth article of the Apostles' Creed is in some sense two articles. (1) He descended into hell. (2) He rose on the third day. Perhaps one reason it seems like two articles is that the first, "he descended into hell," (*descendit ad infernos*) is not found in the earliest versions of the creed. Instead the earliest creeds simply stated that after Jesus died, he rose again on the third day.

Descent into hell

The absence of this phrase in the creed reflects the understanding of one of the earliest creeds of all, one that Paul cites to the Corinthians and we cited in the previous chapter:

> For I handed on to you as of first importance what I also received: that Christ died for our sins in accordance with the scriptures; that he was buried; that he was raised on the third day in accordance with the scriptures; that he appeared to Cephas, then to the Twelve (1 Corinthians 15:3-5).

The absence of the phrase also seems to reflect the understanding that Luke gives us when he relates the conversation between the repentant thief and Jesus:

> Then he said, "Jesus, remember me when you come into your kingdom." He replied to him, "Amen, I say to you, today you will be with me in Paradise" (Luke 23:42-43).

Both the passage from Corinthians and the passage from Luke show no awareness of a descent into hell. On the contrary, according to Luke it appears that after his death Jesus' transit to the Father was immediate. Even in the Gospel of John (20:17), where Jesus says to Mary

Magdalene "Stop holding on to me, for I have not yet ascended to the Father," there is no mention of a descent into hell. The hymn Paul quotes in Philippians also has no mention of hell, or even a descent to the dead (Philippians 2:6-11). There is simply no New Testament evidence of Jesus' descending into hell after his death.[26] (1 Peter 3:19 is a special case, addressed below.)

Indeed, this claim that Christ descended into hell is not even in the earliest versions of the Apostles' Creed. For example, Rufinus, commenting on the creed from Aquilea (cited above), said, "In the creed of the Roman church, we should notice, the words *descended to hell* are not added, nor for that matter does the clause feature in the Eastern churches."[27] We recall that the phrase is not in the baptismal creed from Hippolytus either.

In fact, this creed from Aquilea seems to be the earliest evidence we find for the phrase being added. The phrase in Latin is *descendit ad inferna* translated as "he descended into hell." The Latin term *inferna* literally means "lower parts" but could also mean "the place of the damned." Other Latin texts read *"descendit ad infernos"* which means "he descended to the departed." Thus for the early church, the phrase would have conjured up images of the abode of the dead and only later a fiery hell. The abode of the dead in the lower parts of the world is conveyed by the Hebrew term *sheol*, often translated as *hades* in Greek. The idea of a fiery judgment, or fiery hell, was expressed in the New Testament by the Greek transliteration of the Hebrew term *gehenna*. See the comments on Article Twelve for more about *Sheol* and its background.

The Greek term *gehenna* is ultimately a shortened form of *gê-hinnōm* which means "Valley of Hinnom." This valley marked the northern border of Judah after the return from the Babylonian exile (Nehemiah 11:30). It was the site of child sacrifice, practiced by certain Judeans, not the least of which was the king! (2 Kings 16:3; 21:6; 2 Chronicles

28:3; 33:6). There were so many Judeans killed in this valley in the war with the Babylonians that Jeremiah proclaims that the valley will heretofore be known as the valley of slaughter (Jeremiah 7:29-34; 19:1-5). In the New Testament, the term *gehenna* and other corresponding terms such as *lake of fire and sulphur* describe primarily the fate of the wicked, the devil, and the devil's angels[28] (Matthew 25:41; Revelations 20:10,15; 21:18). Still, *hades* and *gehenna* are distinct, with *hades* representing the abode of the dead and *gehenna* representing the abode of the damned.[29]

So, what are we to make of this phrase, *descended to hell*? Why was it inserted into the creed in the first place? The ancient mind understood the world differently than we do today. In general, ancients conceived of three general regions: heaven (above the earth), the earth, and the region(s) under the earth. God reigned in heaven, human beings lived on the earth, and the dead were in the lower regions of the earth. There are even echoes of this popular cosmology in the New Testament (for example, Ephesians 4:9-10 and Philippians 2:10).

Many Apostolic Fathers expressed the belief that Christ descended to the dead after his own death. We must keep in mind that this is not explicitly stated in the New Testament though there are New Testament passages that lend themselves to this understanding. For example, the Gospel of Matthew has Jesus stating, "Just as Jonah was in the belly of the whale three days and three nights, so will the Son of Man be in the heart of the earth three days and three nights" (Matthew 12:40). Some Apostolic Fathers also articulate a belief in Christ's descent to the dead, for example Ignatius (Magnesians 9) and Polycarp (Philippians 1).

But it was Irenaeus (circa 125-200) who said explicitly that Jesus preached to the departed while he was there:

> And on account of this the Lord descended into the places which are under the earth and proclaimed to them the good news of his

coming, which is the remission of sins received by those who believe in him (*Adversus Haereses,* 4.27.2).

Tertullian (circa 150-230) echoes this belief (*De Anima,* 55) as does Clement of Alexandria (circa 150-216). Yet none of these explicitly cite 1 Peter 3:18-22 which says:

> For Christ also suffered for sins once, the righteous for the sake of the unrighteous, that he might lead you to God. Put to death in the flesh, he was brought to life in the spirit. In it he also went to preach to the spirits in prison, who had once been disobedient while God patiently waited in the days of Noah during the building of the ark, in which a few persons, eight in all, were saved through water. This prefigured baptism, which saves you now. It is not a removal of dirt from the body but an appeal to God for a clear conscience, through the resurrection of Jesus Christ, who has gone into heaven and is at the right hand of God, with angels, authorities, and powers subject to him (1 Peter 3:18-22).

Origen cites this passage explicitly to say that Christ's preaching to those who perished in the deluge is an example of the wicked being saved (*On Principles,* 2.5.3). Most other church fathers, however, do not tie this passage to Christ's descent into hell. That thinking developed much later. Even Augustine wrestled with the proper way to integrate the scripture passage of 1 Peter with the doctrine of descent into hell (Letter 164, to Evodius). Today of course, the church uses 1 Peter 3:19 in support of its teaching that Christ descended into hell (CCC §632) and in that way the doctrine might be an example of the *sensus plenior* (fuller sense) of the scriptural passage. The verse in question is worthy of a fuller treatment below.

Comment on 1 Peter 3:19

Apart from the historical development of the theological idea of Christ's descent into hell, we might ask ourselves what 1 Peter 3:19 meant in its original context. In other words, what did it mean when the ink was wet? Modern scholars maintain that the 1 Peter passage is not about Christ's descent into the dead, much less a descent into hell. For example, in a recent commentary on 1 Peter, John Elliott states clearly:

> The "disobedient spirits in prison" are not deceased humans but the angelic spirits whose disobedience led to the destruction through the Flood, and Christ's announcement entails a confirmation of their eternal condemnation and confinement. The subsequent development of the *descensus* theory and its theological interests should not be allowed to determine or obscure the meaning of 1 Peter 3:19 in its original historical, literary, or theological context.[30]

In fact, Elliott correctly points out that the 1 Peter passage never mentions a descent. Instead, he maintains that the passage in question refers instead to Christ's ascent into heaven (which it does say in 1 Peter 3:22). The doctrine of Christ's descent into hell must therefore have arisen independent of this scriptural passage. Not until the time of Augustine was this link between the descent into hell and 1 Peter 3:19 cemented for later theology.

Finally, let us turn to contemporary interpretations of the theology of Christ's descent. As mentioned above, the writers of the gospels and letters subscribed to the cosmology of their own times, a tripartite cosmology of heaven, earth, and under the earth (cf. Philippians 2:10). Yet how many of us today accept this cosmology at face value? After all, considering the geology of the Earth, we know that we do not find hell underneath us. Instead, below the earth's crust we have the mantle, and eventually the core. Indeed, if it were possible to drill down far enough we would come to the other side of the earth, for the Earth is a sphere. We know this today without even thinking about it. It is a part of our unconscious world view. In the same way, heaven is not up in the sky. The further up we go, the thinner the atmosphere becomes until we reach the exosphere, outer space. Thus, Scripture passages that refer to heaven above and hell below may have been speaking about physical locations above and below us, but we know that those writings were written with a particular world view we no longer share. We can consider the "up" of heaven and the "down" of hell to be metaphorical language. The theology conveyed by the image, rather than the literal image itself, is of critical importance.

In particular, the theology of Christ's descent into hell tells us about the salvific power of Christ's death. That is, the benefits of Christ's death are not limited to those who live after the time of Christ. Christ's death has salvific import for those who were born before Christ because Christ's death and subsequent descent into hell opened heaven for all. Catechetically, we say that while Adam's sin locked the gates of heaven, Christ opened them up again. When Christ descended into hell, he brought up all those who had been denied entrance into heaven, and then opened the gates of heaven for all (cf. CCC § 637).

No less an authority than the late Saint John Paul II recognized this when he said:

> The word of the Gospel and of the Cross reaches all, even those belonging to the most distant past generations; because all who have been saved have been made participants in the Redemption, even before the historical event of Christ's sacrifice on Golgotha happened.... This is the "truth" drawn from the biblical texts cited and which is expressed in the article of the Creed that speaks of "descent into hell."[31]

This understanding is also echoed in the *United States Catholic Catechism for Adults:* "In the language of the early church, this [Jesus descended into hell] meant that Jesus went into the realm of the dead, from which he called out all just people who had lived before him to enter with him into the glory of the Kingdom of Heaven."[32]

So, we recognize that these images of locked gates and opened gates and catechetical expressions emerged from theological speculation, presented in imaginary terms to solve the theological puzzle of the destiny of human beings before Christ.

We might ask ourselves how this applies to the theological challenges of our own day. Often we hear the question like, "What happens to the indigenous person in the deepest forests of the earth who has never heard of Christ?" How do we answer this question? What about all those who have died without ever hearing the name of Jesus? Are they saved? We might think of Christ's descent into hell as the early Church's response to these kinds of questions. Even if some modern people might object to the notion of hell and Christ's descent into it, we recognize that these are metaphorical images used to convey the theological truth that Christ's death has a salvific effect for all humanity.

In summary, the New Testament itself does not directly discuss Christ's descent to the dead, much less his descent into hell. In fact, the idea of Christ's descent into hell is not found in any of the early versions of the creed other than the creed of Aquilea. It seems to have been inserted to address questions regarding the fate of those who died without the benefit of having heard the Gospel message. In this way, the article expresses the salvific effects of what God has done in Christ as extending beyond time and space.

Jesus rose

Turning back to 1 Corinthians, Paul states "that Christ died for our sins in accordance with the scriptures; that he was buried; that he was raised on the third day in accordance with the scriptures; that he appeared to Cephas, then to the Twelve." Here Paul is handing on to the Corinthians what he himself received. Thus, this article of faith, that Jesus rose again on the third day, is certainly of demonstrable apostolic origin.

It is interesting that Paul says Christ was raised on the third day, "in accordance with the scriptures" in parallel construction to Christ's death for our sins "in accordance with the scriptures." We saw above that there is no precise passage in the Old Testament that says the Christ would suffer or even die. Where does it say in the Scriptures that the Messiah would rise on the third day? The short answer is that it does not. Nowhere in the Old Testament is there any mention of the Messiah or anyone else rising on the third day. However, Christians have traditionally pointed to Hosea 6:1-2 as the scriptural reference:

> Come, let us return to the LORD, For it is he who has rent, but he will heal us; he has struck us, but he will bind our wounds. He will revive us after two days; on the third day he will raise us up, to live in his presence (Hosea 6:1-2).

At the same time, no New Testament author explicitly cites Hosea. There are certainly predictions and mentions by various people about Jesus rising on the third day (Matthew 16:21; 17:23; 20:19; Luke 9:22; 18:33; 24:7, 21, 46) or after three days (Matthew 12:40; 27:63; Mark 8:31; 9:31; 10:34). There are faith statements that God raised Jesus or Jesus was raised on the third day (Acts 10:40; 1 Corinthians 15:4). In Matthew, the soldiers are ordered to secure the tomb until the third day, lest his disciples come and steal the body (27:64). There is a Lucan story in which Jesus says, "and on the third day I accomplish my purpose" (13:32). And of course there are the temple predictions, seen in light of resurrection, "Destroy this temple and in three days I will raise it up" (cf. Matthew 26:61; 27:40; Mark 14:58; 15:29; John 2:19). But perhaps nowhere is the claim so bold as in Luke 24:46, "Thus it is written that the Messiah would suffer and rise from the dead on the third day." The New Testament authors are content to say that Jesus rose on the third day, and some might even add, "according to the Scriptures" without citing any particular passage. By making this claim, they were able to maintain that the resurrection of Jesus fulfilled Scripture.

Resurrection, or Jesus' rising from the dead, is perhaps the central tenet of Christianity. Had the apostles not proclaimed that Jesus rose from the dead, Jesus would perhaps have been understood as merely a good teacher who met a violent end. As it stands, the apostles proclaimed the Easter message, "The Lord has truly been raised" (Luke 24:34) and "I have seen the Lord" (John 20:18, 25; 1 Corinthians 9:1). This apostolic preaching formed the basis of the church. As Paul tells the Corinthians, "Therefore, whether it be I or they, so we preach and so you believed" (1 Corinthians 15:11). And thus it has continued through the centuries. The Easter message is proclaimed anew each Easter Sunday, each weekly Sunday, and indeed each day of the year. "So we preach and so you believed." Because the apostles believed and preached, we too believe and preach.

About ten years ago, news headlines announced the discovery of the supposed tomb of Jesus, perhaps containing the bones of Jesus himself. What to make of such a find? A better question might be, what would the apostles have thought about the tomb of Jesus where his corpse lay? Would they have preached had the bones of Jesus indeed been situated in an ossuary in Jerusalem? Christianity is an apostolic faith. That is, Christian faith is built on the faith of the apostles. The apostles believed and taught that Jesus rose from the dead. If, at the time of the apostles' preaching, there were an ossuary containing Jesus' bones, one might simply deny the Easter message by pointing to those same bones. It is perhaps in recognition of this fact that the Gospel of Matthew mentions Pilate stationing guards lest the disciples steal the body and claim that Jesus rose (Matthew 27:62-66). As the story goes, the tomb was empty, and the apostles proclaimed that Jesus rose. Faith or unbelief are the only two responses.

Put simply, one either believes in the resurrection and is a Christian or does not believe and as a result is not Christian. Or perhaps like Thomas, we say, "Unless I see the mark of the nails in his hands and put my finger into the nailmarks and put my hand into his side, I will not believe" (John 20:25). Some early Christians must have shared this sentiment, since the evangelist records the words on the lips of Jesus, "Blessed are those who have not seen and have believed" (John 20:29b). Paul, too, alludes to this skeptical sentiment when he asks:

...how can some among you say there is no resurrection of the dead? If there is no resurrection of the dead, then neither has Christ been raised. And if Christ has not been raised, then empty (too) is our preaching; empty, too, your faith (1 Corinthians 15:12b-14).

Clearly, not all Christians could accept the resurrection. Even 2 Timothy mentions "Hymenaeus and Philetus, who have deviated from the truth by saying that (the) resurrection has already taken place and are upsetting the faith of some" (2 Timothy 2:17b-18).

In some ways, the same challenges that faced the early Christians face us. The New Testament itself attests that some of the claims made today — that the disciples stole the body of Jesus, or that belief in the resurrection is unnecessary — were made at the time of the apostles, too. Paul gave no demonstrable proof of the resurrection of Jesus other than his eyewitness testimony and the reports about the eyewitness testimony of others (1 Corinthians 15:3-8). Ultimately, the same "proof" offered to the Corinthians is offered to us today. The apostolic preaching — "I have seen the Lord" — engages us. We cannot see the Lord as the apostles did. But we can listen to the preaching of the apostles and choose to believe or not. This is the same option given to the first generation of Christians at Corinth. The choice that faced them faces us.

THE BOTTOM LINE

Christ's death released all from the power of death, making salvation available to everyone, regardless of time and space. Christ's resurrection was God's definitive affirmation of Jesus Christ. By the resurrection, Jesus conquered death once and for all and gave humanity a glimpse into the future that awaits us. The resurrection of Christ remains a central tenet of Christianity.

DISCUSSION QUESTIONS

Refer to *Catechism of the Catholic Church,* §631-658.

- Where is the risen Christ now? Explain your answer

- Why does it matter to you that Jesus rose from the dead?

- Though the creed says Jesus rose from the dead, many New Testament passages say that God raised Jesus from the dead. Do you see any difference? Does it matter to you?

- Is Christ's descent into hell a meaningful doctrine for you? Why or why not?

Article Six

He ascended into heaven
and is seated at the right hand of the Father.

The previous chapter recognized that the gospels use metaphorical language when talking about Christ's descent into hell. The theological take-away from that metaphorical language was that salvation is available to all. In the present article of the Apostles' Creed, we encounter yet more metaphorical language speaking of Christ's ascent into heaven. One difference between the descent into hell and the ascent into heaven is that, unlike in the case of the descent, the Scriptures do explicitly mention the ascension, especially Luke (24:50-53), Acts (1:6-12), and John (20:17).

Old Testament

The Old Testament provides a rich background for understanding the concept of ascension into heaven, which essentially means ascension to the realm of God. For example, Enoch is said to have walked with God (Genesis 5:24) and Elijah is taken to heaven in a fiery chariot (2 Kings 2:1-18). Coronation psalms speak of the king being seated at the right hand of God (Psalms 24, 47, 68, especially 110; cf. also 118). All of these serve as a background to understanding ascension language. In ancient cultures the one seated on the right of the host enjoyed special favor. Thus, to be seated at God's right means to enjoy the favor and power of God, as the psalms indicate. In the Old Testament, the king was said to enjoy this special favor of God.

New Testament

The New Testament ascension stories of Jesus confirm the resurrection appearances and in some cases combine both into one. The ascension of Jesus can be understood as his final leave-taking before his assembled followers. After his ascension Jesus will no longer appear to his disciples as he once did. The ascension in effect answers the believer's question: Where is the risen Lord now? The answer is that he has ascended to heaven.

Only Luke in his gospel and in Acts gives us a narrative of the ascension of Jesus. Other New Testament authors simply assume it or make some reference to it. For example, the great Christological hymn of Philippians speaks simply of the exaltation of Christ (2:9); 1 Peter 3:22 mentions Christ "gone into heaven"; and 1 Timothy 3:16 expresses something similar in saying he was "taken up in glory."

Heaven itself is a metaphor for the otherworldly presence or dwelling place of God. In antiquity, the dwelling place of God was understood to be up above. Thus, if Jesus goes to God, he ascends.

As this is metaphorical language, we recognize that the heavens are not really "up." We recall that the ancient mind understood the earth and the heavens differently than we do today. A careful reading of Genesis 1 tells us that there is a firmament, or dome, in the sky separating the heavens from the earth. This is also reflected in other Old Testament passages such as Psalm 19:2; Job 37:18. Above the dome is where God kept his storerooms for rain, ice, snow, and so forth (Job 37:6; 38:22-23). The earth itself was thought to be a disk surrounded by the oceans. Of course, we don't understand the world in this way today. A literal reading of Genesis 1 would discourage a modern person from sending a rocket into outer space, since it would crash into the dome! Today, we have an entirely different cosmology.

Modern Preconceptions

The modern understanding of the world recognizes the earth as a sphere, which rotates on its own axis (to give us day and night) and which revolves around the sun (to give us seasons and years). Ancient Greek thinkers (as opposed to the biblical authors) knew the earth was a sphere. For one, they had taken notice of the shadow of the earth when it passed over the moon during an eclipse. Also, having made precise measurements of shadows cast by the midday sun at different latitudes, they were able to determine the circumference of the earth's sphere. Though the ancient Greeks understood the earth was a sphere, they did not believe it rotated on its own axis or revolved around the sun. They had considered these as possibilities, but they ultimately dismissed them for what at the time were good scientific reasons.[33]

Of course, today we take for granted the fact that the earth is a sphere, rotates on its axis, and revolves around the sun. We travel in airplanes seven miles high, far above some clouds. We distinguish between the troposphere, the stratosphere, the mesosphere, the thermosphere, and the exosphere. Satellites travel through space in geosynchronous orbit. The moon itself is a satellite orbiting the earth. If we travel high enough with enough power, we would not hit the dome imagined in Genesis 1, but we would escape earth's gravitational pull and experience weightlessness, with the vast expanse of the universe all around us, our view unimpeded by the earth's atmosphere.

In fact, if we were to point straight up into the sky at any given time of the day and then point up again at the sky twelve hours later, we would be pointing at different sides of the sky and at completely different parts of the universe. In other words, noon at one point on the globe is a different sky than midnight at the same point on the globe. Only the daytime sky with its bright sun overpowers the stars we might see at that point. The ancient mind did not understand the world in this way, and thus we see references in the Scriptures to domes, firmaments, and heavens above.

What does it mean then for Christians to proclaim Christ's ascent into heaven? Someone taking biblical descriptions literally might ask, "How far up into the sky did he ultimately go?" or "Did he go only so far up as to move beyond the ability of human vision, then vanish?" Such questions do not respect the fundamental point, however, that the Scriptures express theological truths not literally but through metaphor.

THE BOTTOM LINE

Ascension into heaven means that Christ lives now with God, at God's right hand, exalted to glory. Christ enjoys the favor of God, and shares in God's power.

DISCUSSION QUESTIONS

Refer to *Catechism of the Catholic Church,* §659-667.

- What other metaphors might we use today to express the same fundamental truth expressed by Jesus' ascension into heaven?

- Given that Jesus shares in the power of God, how do you experience his power in your own life?

- Did Jesus share in the power of God during his earthly life? Do you do so now? If so, what might be different about the heavenly power he enjoys now?

ANCIENT FAITH FOR THE MODERN WORLD

Article Seven

From there he will come
to judge the living and the dead.

To say that Jesus Christ, God's only Son, our Lord, will come again pre-supposes that he, the Messiah, came once already. This belief was, however, a sticking point between early Jews and Christians. It was clear to the early Christians that Jesus was humble in death. (Philippians 2:7-8; cf. Acts 8:33). He was, as the prophet says, like the lamb being led to the slaughter. The Jews of Jesus' day, however, were expecting not a weak, submissive, suffering, and crucified Messiah, and thus interpreted Jesus' death on a cross as proof that he was not the Messiah. Jews of Jesus' day were generally expecting a Messiah who would be a powerful ruler, trampling foes, restoring the kingdom, and leading an age of peace. The reason for this is that, although the Old Testament does have passages referring to the sacrificial lamb and the suffering servant, these passages are not the same as those referring to a Messiah. In short, the Old Testament does not say the suffering servant and the Messiah were one and the same. Christians made that claim based on their experience of the risen Christ. Their experience of the Lord Jesus, raised from the dead, enabled Christians to recognize the Messiahship of Jesus despite his not conforming to this expected pattern.

The experience of the risen Christ shattered many preconceived notions and reset the deck, so to speak, so that the Sacred Scriptures were read anew in light of the resurrection. The early Christians drew new connections in reading Scripture that were heretofore unseen. Since Jesus was both the Messiah and the one who suffered and died on the cross, it was "easy" to forge the two into the image of a suffering Messiah. Jewish readers of the Scriptures, without an experience of the risen Christ, would not have and even could not have read Scripture as the Christians did.

The second part of the seventh article of the Apostles' Creed states that, having come once, Jesus will come again to judge the living and the dead. There are two parts to this assertion: the first that Jesus will come again and the second that Jesus will come as judge. The belief in the coming again of Jesus Christ, the Lord, is ancient. In fact, one of the prayers that Paul preserves for us in Aramaic is simply one word, *maranatha*, which means "Come, our lord" (1 Corinthians 16:22b). Because of the Aramaic phrase preserved in this passage, scholars date the passage, and thus the Christian faith in the Lord's coming, to the earliest days of the Christian community, perhaps before even the conversion of Paul. The second part of the article — that Jesus will come again to judge — deserves further discussion. In his humble submission to death on the cross, Jesus did not act as judge. Early Christians maintained that Jesus would come again, only this time appearing as judge of humanity, the living and the dead. (See 2 Timothy 4:1,8; 1 Peter 4:5.) Let us explore the Old and New Testament roots of this belief.

Old Testament

In the Old Testament, the power to judge belongs to God alone (for example, 1 Samuel 2:10; Psalms 96:10,13; 98:9; 110:6; Isaiah 33:22; Ezekiel 7:27; 24:14; 35:11). Judgment is often meted out based on a person's actions. Frequently in biblical texts we hear the voice of those who are maltreated or treated with injustice. For example, Amos (2:6-7; 4:1; 5:12; 8:4-6) decries the rich who gain their wealth on the backs of the poor. In these cases, the oppressed have no one to turn to but God. God is said to have a concern for the poor, the widowed, and the orphan precisely because these people are often oppressed, without recourse to justice. Thus, God is presented as acting on their behalf, meting out justice, and protecting the basic human rights of all.

New Testament

In the New Testament there are passages that state clearly that God will judge (for example, Romans 3:6; 1 Peter 2:12; Hebrews 12:23), but there

ANCIENT FAITH FOR THE MODERN WORLD

are others that give Jesus a role in that judgment. For example, Paul says that God through Jesus will judge the secret thoughts of all (Romans 2:16).[34] In many other New Testament passages the power to judge on the last day is related to Jesus. For example, in the Gospel of Matthew, Jesus describes the eschatological judgment with the metaphor of separating sheep from goats. In this parable those who have treated the poor and outcast of the world with kindness and loving care are rewarded, for in so doing they were showing kindness and loving care to Jesus himself. On the other hand those who neglected the care of the poor were condemned for neglecting Jesus (Matthew 25:31-46).

The fact that both the living and the dead will be judged conjures up images from the famous parable of Lazarus and the rich man in Luke:

There was a rich man who dressed in purple garments and fine linen and dined sumptuously each day. And lying at his door was a poor man named Lazarus, covered with sores, who would gladly have eaten his fill of the scraps that fell from the rich man's table. Dogs even used to come and lick his sores. When the poor man died, he was carried away by angels to the bosom of Abraham. The rich man also died and was buried, and from the netherworld, where he was in torment, he raised his eyes and saw Abraham far off and Lazarus at his side. And he cried out, 'Father Abraham, have pity on me. Send Lazarus to dip the tip of his finger in water and cool my tongue, for I am suffering torment in these flames.' Abraham replied, 'My child, remember that you received what was good during your lifetime while Lazarus likewise received what was bad; but now he is comforted here, whereas you are tormented (Luke 16:19-25).

In this story the traditional roles of rich and poor are reversed —

a Lucan theme, as seen for example in the Magnificat (Luke 1:51-53). Those who enjoyed the good things of this world will weep in the after-life, whereas those who weep now will rejoice (cf. Luke 6:20-26). There will be a coming judgment.

In addition to God judging in the Old Testament and that power being vested in Jesus when he comes again, Paul seems to have had little difficulty in encouraging his community to judge. Here we are not talking about the cataclysmic apocalyptic judgment at the end of the age but the simple day to day judgment or discernment that occurs almost by necessity in the life of a community. Paul is scandalized that the Corinthians are celebrating a man living with his stepmother as though they are married. Paul says that such a thing is not found even among the Gentiles. He decries their attitude and wonders if they had not read his earlier letter wherein he warned them not to associate with immoral people. For Paul, the community was to be holy, that is, set apart for service to God. Those Christians who were boldly living immoral lives were to be excluded (1 Corinthians 5:1-13).

Yet this advice from Paul needs to be balanced with gospel stories of forgiveness and reconciliation. Perhaps the most famous of these stories is that of the woman caught in adultery.

> Then the scribes and the Pharisees brought a woman who had been caught in adultery and made her stand in the middle. They said to him, "Teacher, this woman was caught in the very act of committing adultery. Now in the law, Moses commanded us to stone such women. So what do you say?" They said this to test him, so that they could have some charge to bring against him. Jesus bent down and began to write on the ground with his finger. But when they continued asking him, he straightened up and said to them, "Let the one among you who is without sin be

the first to throw a stone at her." Again he bent down and wrote on the ground. And in response, they went away one by one, beginning with the elders. So he was left alone with the woman before him. Then Jesus straightened up and said to her, "Woman, where are they? Has no one condemned you?" She replied, "No one, sir." Then Jesus said, "Neither do I condemn you. Go, (and) from now on do not sin any more" (John 8:3-11).

Balancing the desire to lead a holy life with the command to forgive is something worked out by each Christian in his or her daily life.

Thus the creed concludes the articles about Jesus. The articles began with Jesus being called Christ. The articles about Jesus mention the incarnation but neglect the public ministry. They mention the passion, death, resurrection, and ascension, and neglect Jesus' miracles but mention his future coming as judge. Half of the articles of the Apostles' Creed deal directly with Jesus, though nowhere do we read about his presence in the Eucharist, the other sacraments, or the liturgical life of the church. The Creed does not have any ethical directives or commands.

THE BOTTOM LINE

There will be a final judgment of all humanity. Death does not preclude one from being judged. Christ himself will judge when he comes again.

DISCUSSION QUESTIONS

Refer to *Catechism of the Catholic Church,* §668-682.

- How are you called to act in light of the parables Jesus teaches about judgment? Give examples.

- How comfortable are you with a judging Jesus? Why?

- If you were to be judged now, how would you fare? Explain.

- How do you square the judgment of Jesus with the claim that God wants to save all?

Article Eight

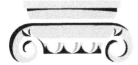

I believe in the Holy Spirit...

Catholics begin each Mass by making the sign of the cross "in the name of the Father and of the Son and of the Holy Spirit." The third person of the Trinity is the object of belief in the eighth article of the Apostles' Creed, which begins with "I believe in...." The Holy Spirit is understood by Christians to be the creative presence of God in the world. It might surprise some to find that the "spirit of God," and even the Holy Spirit itself, is mentioned in the Old Testament, where it often refers to the dynamic, creative presence of God in the community, in the world, or in an individual.

Old Testament

In the Hebrew Old Testament, the word most often translated as spirit is *rûāh*, whose basic meaning is "wind," or "breath." The term can also refer to the inner disposition and volition of a human being. One's *rûāh* is able to be moved by God.

When *rûāh* is used of God, it means the creative, life-giving, prophetic, energizing power of God in the life of the individual and the community.[35] When the term *rûāh YHWH*[36] or *rûāh elohim*[37] occurs, the meaning is generally "spirit" in the sense that the concepts wind and breath have been overshadowed and something even more intangible is meant (for example, Psalm 139:7). Furthermore, *rûāh YHWH* is associated with the early leadership of Israel by Yahweh that includes deliverance from Egypt, various military actions, prophetic leadership through individuals,[38] and ecstatic prophecy.[39] In biblical literature of a later period, *rûāh* no longer specifies a particular divine act; but rather, it simply refers to God. Often, the noun *qodesh* (holy) is also applied. For example, Isaiah 63:10-11 states, "But they rebelled, and grieved his holy spirit; So he turned to become their enemy, and warred against them. Then they remembered the days of old, of Moses, his servant: Where is he who brought up out of the sea the shepherd of his flock?

Where is he who placed in their midst his holy spirit...." Or again, "Do not drive me from before your face, nor take from me your holy spirit" (Psalm 51:13).

New Testament

Because of that history, the Holy Spirit was not a concept introduced only in the New Testament. Instead, the first Christians, who were themselves Jews, used the terminology and names for God's presence as they had available to reflect their belief. The Holy Spirit, which was the Old Testament's way to speak of God's dynamic presence in the world, was the same dynamic presence of God they saw active in Jesus' life and in the life of the early Christian community. If one were to ask a first century Jewish Christian, "How was Jesus raised?" the answer would be, "by the power of the Holy Spirit," or "by the spirit of him who raised Jesus from the dead." That is, Jesus was raised by the dynamic, powerful, creative presence of God.

In like fashion, if one were to ask a first century Jewish Christian, "How was Jesus conceived?" the answer might be, "by the power of the Holy Spirit," for Luke says, "the power of the most high will overshadow you," which in effect means that the Holy Spirit will come upon you. That is, Jesus is conceived by the dynamic, powerful, creative presence of God. The early Christians did not invent the term *holy spirit*. It was a term familiar to them from their Scriptures, what Christians today call the Old Testament.

Spirit in Paul's Letters

Paul contributes much to the Christian understanding of Holy Spirit. Paul, writing in Greek, uses the term *pneuma* (spirit) 120 times[40] and *psychē* (soul) eleven times.[41] These numbers alone indicate that *soul* is not a primary element of discussion for Paul. Rather, he writes about *spirit*. The debates in classical Greek literature over the nature of the human soul (*psychē*) are absent from Paul. Plato and Aristotle themselves did not agree on the question of the soul. On the one hand, Plato maintained that the body was a tomb for the immortal soul so that when the body died the soul would be free to live forever unencumbered by the body. On the other hand, Aristotle held that the soul was the form of the body and once the body died the soul died with it. Rather than engage the philosophers of classical Greece, Paul engages the world around him wearing Old Testament lenses ground by his experience of the resurrected Christ. Paul never speaks of the human being as body and soul. In fact, the entire New Testament scarcely uses that term for the human being. Yet Paul uses the term *spirit* both anthropologically and theologically. Anthropologically, Paul usually means by *pneuma* "that aspect of a human being which is the knowing and willing self. As such, it expresses what is especially apt to receive the Spirit of God (Romans 1:9; 8:16)."[42] As distinct from the non-Christian Greek usage, which uses the word *pneuma* to speak of ecstatic and rapturous powers, Paul uses *spirit* theologically and reflects much of the Old Testament concept of Spirit of God or *rûāh*. Even more than this, however, in Paul God's creative, life-giving, prophetic, energizing power in the life of an individual and the community is brought to the Christian by Jesus Christ: "the Lord is the Spirit" (2 Corinthians 3:17).[43]

Paul never directly says that Christ *is* the Spirit of God, although he uses interchangeably the terms *Spirit of God; Spirit of Christ; Christ, the Spirit of him who raised Jesus from the dead;* and *his Spirit* (Romans 8:9-11). Some scholars see triadic language in 1 Corinthians 12:4-6:

There are different kinds of spiritual gifts but the same Spirit;

there are different forms of service but the same Lord;

there are different workings but the same God who produces all of them in everyone.

Here Paul clearly is using the word *Lord* to refer to Jesus. The question is whether *Spirit, Lord,* and *God* are three ways of referring to God or some other meaning that Paul intends. A better example of Paul clearly distinguishing a triad is in 2 Corinthians 13:13 which we echo in the liturgy: "The grace of the Lord Jesus Christ and the love of God and the fellowship of the holy Spirit be with all of you." Paul's theology, specifically the relationship between God, Jesus, and the Holy Spirit, is not precise. Instead, his theology is functional: He is interested in what Christ has done for the salvation of human beings and how human beings respond to that gift. (I use the word *triad* here rather than *Trinity*, because *Trinity* is a Latin-based word that carries with it all the baggage of later theological debates. The point is that Paul's language is triadic, which will give rise to later Latin-speaking theologians who forge Trinitarian theology based on these and other texts.)

The Spirit itself intercedes for Christians (Romans 8:26); it is the source of their adoption by God (Romans 8:15) and their freedom (2 Corinthians 3:17). As the *Theological Dictionary of the New Testament* puts it:

> For Paul the Spirit of God is not an odd power which works magically; the Spirit reveals to the believer God's saving work in Christ and makes possible his understanding and responsible acceptance thereof.... For this reason the pneuma, though always God's Spirit and never evaporating into the pneuma given individually to man, is also the innermost ego of the one who no longer lives by his own being but by God's being for him.[44]

ANCIENT FAITH FOR THE MODERN WORLD

In 1 Corinthians 2:11-13, Paul compares and contrasts the Spirit of God in a variety of ways:

Among human beings, who knows what pertains to a person except the spirit of the person that is within? Similarly, no one knows what pertains to God except the Spirit of God. We have not received the spirit of the world but the Spirit that is from God, so that we may understand the things freely given us by God. And we speak about them not with words taught by human wisdom but with words taught by the Spirit, describing spiritual realities in spiritual terms.

In 1 Corinthians 2:11, Paul draws a parallel between the Spirit of God and the human spirit,[45] but in the following verse he contrasts, in a way recalling what he said a few verses earlier,[46] the spirit of the world with the Spirit that is from God. The contrast he draws in 1 Corinthians 2:13 also spells out the difference between the Spirit and human wisdom, or the wisdom of this age. The wisdom of this age is in marked contrast to the wisdom of God, which Christians know as a result of their having received the Spirit of God. Later in this letter Paul illustrates the union to be had with the Lord in terms of spirit: "But whoever is joined to the Lord becomes one spirit with him" (1 Corinthians 6:17).

Paul also uses *pneuma* as juxtaposed to either *sarx* — flesh — or *sōma* — body. In doing so Paul contrasts the human being dominated by selfish desires (flesh), with the human being open to receiving the Spirit of God:

...so that the righteous decree of the law might be fulfilled in us, who live not according to the flesh but according to the spirit. For those who live according to the flesh are concerned with the things of the flesh, but those who live according to the spirit with the things of the spirit. The concern of the flesh is death, but the concern of the spirit is life and peace. For the concern of the flesh is hostility toward God; it does not submit to the law of God, nor can it; and those who are in the flesh cannot please God. But you are not in the flesh; on the contrary, you are in the spirit, if only the Spirit of God dwells in you. Whoever does not have the Spirit of Christ does not belong to him.... For if you live according to the flesh, you will die, but if by the spirit you put to death the deeds of the body, you will live (Romans 8:4-9,13).

For Paul, humanity was bound by its self-interested desires, that is, a life according to the flesh. The law was then imposed on humanity and pointed out what was forbidden. However, the law did not give humanity the power to follow the law's precepts. Simply by pointing out what was forbidden, the law stirred up in humanity the desire to do what was forbidden. In Paul's view, that situation was changed by the Christ event. The Spirit gives Christians the power to live. Those who live according to the flesh are those whose lives are dominated by self-centered interests, carnal pursuits, and carnal thoughts.[47] However, to live according to the Spirit means that *sarx* does not rule over us, much less dominate our perspective. Instead, we are ruled by the Spirit of God. The striving of one led by *sarx* is death; the striving of one led by the Spirit of God is life and peace. Those dominated by flesh are hostile to God and cannot be submissive to God's law. The self-absorbed cannot please God. Paul reminds his Christian readers that they do not share the condition of sinful humanity; they are not self-absorbed. God's Spirit dwells in them. By that Spirit, Christians can put to death selfish and carnal inclinations and instead truly live.

In his letter to the Galatians, Paul juxtaposes flesh and Spirit in two

ANCIENT FAITH FOR THE MODERN WORLD

ways. Paul shows that trusting in circumcision, or works of the flesh, does not offer salvation. Instead, salvation comes about by faith: "But just as then the child of the flesh persecuted the child of the spirit, it is the same now" (Galatians 4:29). Paul refers here to Abraham's two sons.[48] Those born according to the flesh (here Ishmael, but also the Jews) persecute those born according to the Spirit (Isaac, but also the Christians). The distinction is between those who now place their hope in the flesh (circumcision) and those who place their faith in the promised Spirit (Galatians 4:23).

Though both passages illustrate a theological meaning, the use of *flesh* and *Spirit* in Galatians 4 is slightly different from that expressed in Galatians 5:16-17: "I say, then: live by the Spirit and you will certainly not gratify the desire of the flesh. For the flesh has desires against the Spirit, and the Spirit against the flesh; these are opposed to each other, so that you may not do what you want." In chapter 4 Paul shows that God's plan of salvation is by faith rather than by the law. In chapter 5 Paul contrasts two ways of living, but both passages have a theological meaning.

Paul continues the theological distinction of these terms in Galatians 6: "...because the one who sows for his flesh will reap corruption from the flesh, but the one who sows for the spirit will reap eternal life from the spirit" (Galatians 6:8). The gist of this verse is essentially that of Romans 8:4-9,13, even to the point of similarly balanced phrases.[49] The way of flesh leads to death, but the Spirit leads to eternal life.

Thus, when Paul contrasts flesh and Spirit, he generally means by *flesh* a human way of life motivated by selfish desires, or earthbound carnal tendencies, while by *Spirit* he means a human life open to the activity of God's Spirit leading to eternal life.

In summary, Paul uses *pneuma* anthropologically to mean that aspect of the human being receptive to the influence of God. Theologically his use of *pneuma* is akin to that of the Old Testament, that is, to express the creative, life-giving power of God at work in an individual or the community. Theologically, Paul contrasts *pneuma* with *sarx* when he wants to indicate humanity cooperating with God as opposed to humanity's pursuit of its own "selfish desires."

Spirit in Mark's Gospel

In Mark, the first gospel to have been composed, we hear the story of Jesus' baptism: "It happened in those days that Jesus came from Nazareth of Galilee and was baptized in the Jordan by John. On coming up out of the water he saw the heavens being torn open and the Spirit, like a dove, descending upon him" (Mark 1:9-10). Note that the text does not say that the Spirit *was* a dove; but rather, the Spirit descended *like* a dove. Moreover, Jesus himself saw the Spirit descend in this way.

The identification of the Spirit descending like a dove finds no parallel in the Old Testament. Some will propose a symbolic meaning of a new creation and find a parallel in Genesis 1:2 where the spirit of God hovers over the waters, but there is no mention of dove. Others will propose a symbolic meaning of deliverance, redemption, or peace and find a parallel in Genesis 8:8, where Noah releases a dove; but in Genesis 8:8 there is no mention of Spirit. Ultimately, Mark is saying that the ministry of Jesus is inaugurated by the outpouring of the Spirit on him, much like figures in the Old Testament.

Spirit in Luke's Gospel

Luke, who used the Gospel of Mark as a source, has shaped the story differently:

> After all the people had been baptized and Jesus also had been baptized and was praying, heaven was opened and the holy Spir-

it descended upon him in bodily form like a dove. And a voice came from heaven, "You are my beloved Son; with you I am well pleased" (Luke 3:21-22).

Luke makes clear that many people were being baptized, and that Jesus was one of the many. Moreover, the verb is in the perfect tense of the passive voice: "when Jesus also had been baptized." Luke also adds the note about Jesus praying, a favorite Lucan theme. He adds two adjectives: *Holy* to Spirit, again reflecting his interests, and *sōmatikō(i)*, meaning "in bodily form," which occurs only here in the entire New Testament. The latter adjective is used by Luke most likely to show the tangible reality of the event. Luke does something similar in the resurrection appearance narrative when the risen Lord says, "Look at my hands and my feet, that it is I myself. Touch me and see, because a ghost does not have flesh and bones as you can see I have" (Luke 24:39).

God's spirit is a prominent Lucan theme — or rather, character — in Luke and Acts, who is ever at work in the entire narrative. The spirit is at work in the prophets. It is by God's spirit that Mary conceives. Jesus is baptized and thus receives the spirit. The spirit empowers Jesus' own ministry. The spirit is a gift of God given not only to Jesus but also at Pentecost to the assembled believers. Thus the spirit guides the early church through its initial difficulties, including the decision to lay hands on seven men to assist with the daily distribution. Also, the spirit is given freely by God to Cornelius and his household to such a degree that Peter considers that he would be fighting God himself if he had withheld baptism. So, the spirit is ultimately guiding the entire narrative, from the conception of Jesus, through the ministry of Jesus, to the outpouring of the spirit at Pentecost, including the decision to accept Gentiles without circumcision.

Spirit in Matthew's Gospel

The spirit of God is also prominent in the Gospel of Matthew, who gives us the story of the Great Commission, with its famous triadic text:

> "Go, therefore, and make disciples of all nations, baptizing them in the name of the Father, and of the Son, and of the holy Spirit, teaching them to observe all that I have commanded you. And behold, I am with you always, until the end of the age" (Matthew 28:19-20).

In fact, it is from this text that the Church receives the baptismal formula it uses to this very day.

> N., I baptize you in the name of the Father, and of the Son, and of the Holy Spirit.[50]

Spirit in John's Gospel

We would be remiss not to mention the Gospel of John, which conveys a slightly different theology of the Holy Spirit, but one completely congruent of course with the rest of the New Testament. John calls the Spirit the *Advocate*, or *Paraclete*. This language conjures up images of a legal assistant, or attorney. In fact, there are four Advocate sayings in the Gospel of John, the first of which occurs in 14:16-17:

> And I will ask the Father, and he will give you another Advocate to be with you always, the Spirit of truth, which the world cannot accept, because it neither sees nor knows it. But you know it, because it remains with you, and will be in you.

This is the first of four "advocate" sayings at the Last Supper discourse (the others are 14:25-26; 15:25-26; 16:7-15). The advocate, or paraclete, is a helper, someone at one's side. We see from this saying that Jesus was the first advocate. The Father will give them another. The second advocate, the Spirit of truth, has been interpreted as the presence of Jesus after his death and resurrection. Thus, when in the story, Jesus promises not to leave them orphans, that he is coming back, the evangelist means that Jesus himself is coming to them as the advocate.

In the second advocate saying we encounter the only instance in which the Paraclete is called "holy spirit." The Spirit will teach them all things and remind them of what Jesus himself taught. The Spirit is related to the earthly Jesus.

The relationship between Jesus and the Father becomes the model for the relationship between the Spirit and Jesus. Jesus sends the spirit in 15:26-27. In the last advocate saying, the Paraclete has a function vis-à-vis the world. The Paraclete, almost like a prosecuting attorney, convicts the world with respect to three things: sin, righteousness, and judgment. Thus, the Paraclete has both an internal and external function. The internal function concerns the life of the church, calling to mind the teachings of Jesus. The external function witnesses to the world and convicts the world.

Clear expressions of a well formulated doctrine of the Trinity are basically nonexistent in the New Testament. Instead we have texts speaking of God in triadic terms (especially 2 Corinthians 13:13 and Matthew 28:19-20). This is not to say that the doctrine of the Trinity is unfounded or has no New Testament support. The roots of the doctrine of the Trinity are certainly found in the New Testament. But as we saw above, *Trinity* is a Latin-based word not found in the New Testament; it is not even found in the creed. Theologians wrestled for centuries over how best to speak of the mystery of God, the identity of Jesus, Jesus' relationship to God, the relationship of God's Spirit to Jesus, etc. Even today, many

Christians think of the Trinity as two men and a dove, which is a gross simplification. It is difficult to express what theologians mean by Trinity in pictures, as there is always more that is dissimilar to the dogmatic theological ideal than is similar, but artists continue to make attempts.

Andrei Rublev (1360-1430) was a Russian iconographer whose "Trinity" (or "Hospitality of Abraham") has captured the imagination of untold millions. In the icon, Rublev portrays three persons sharing a meal. The scene conjures up thoughts of Genesis 18:1-18, in which three angels visit Abraham and Sarah. Yet in the icon there is no Abraham, no Sarah, only the three visitors. They are portrayed as co-equal, and in communion, or in relationship. This icon then represents for many a different way of imagining Trinity.

Balancing a careful articulation of monotheism with three "persons" is difficult. *Person* of course was the language forged in the heat of theological battle over a millennium ago, and it is used in a highly philosophical and technical sense, not the way we commonly use the term today. Rather than separate "beings," it is more helpful to think of the three persons as three "centers of consciousness" or "three freedoms." For example, the church uses the term *person* to distinguish Father, Son, and Spirit but the term *nature* to express the unity of the divine. The three persons of the Trinity share one divine nature. Yet this language has been problematic and difficult to explain throughout the centuries. The Qur'an, for example, blasts the notion of three persons in one God:

> People of the Book, go not beyond the bounds in your religion, and say not as to God but the truth. The Messiah, Jesus son of Mary, was only the Messenger of God, and His Word that He committed to Mary, and a Spirit from Him. So believe in God and His Messengers, and say not, 'Three.' Refrain; better is it for you. God is only One God. Glory be to Him — That He should

ANCIENT FAITH FOR THE MODERN WORLD

have a son! To Him belongs all that is in the heavens and in the earth; God suffices for a guardian (4.171).

And in a later passage:

They are unbelievers who say, "God is the Third of Three." No god is there but One God. If they refrain not from what they say, there shall afflict those of them that disbelieve a painful chastisement (5.73).

Certainly Christians today profess belief in the Holy Spirit. Yet even this article of the creed does not say the "Holy Spirit is God." Instead, the article is introduced by the verb, "I believe" which also introduced the first and second article. In that way, belief in the Father, the Son, and the Holy Spirit are on par with one another. Later councils and later creeds, more fully articulate this belief in the Spirit, adding phrases like, "The Lord, the Giver of Life."

THE BOTTOM LINE

The Holy Spirit is the creative, dynamic, powerful presence of God in the world and in the lives of all people. This is the same spirit that hovered over the waters (Genesis 1:2), was spoken of in the Psalms (Psalm 51:13), raised Jesus from the dead (Romans 8:11), and animates the lives of Christians through the centuries, down to this very day. The Spirit is life-giving.

DISCUSSION QUESTIONS

Refer to *Catechism of the Catholic Church,* §683-747.

- How meaningful is the Holy Spirit in your own life? Explain.

- How do you experience God the Holy Spirit distinct from God the Father or God the Son, Jesus Christ?

- How have you experienced the power of the Holy Spirit in your life? Give examples.

Article Nine

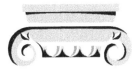

The holy catholic Church,
the communion of saints...

The ninth article of the Apostles' Creed moves away from the persons of the Trinity and toward the community of believers: the holy catholic church and the communion of saints. The articles concerning each person of the godhead each began with "I believe in...." With this ninth article, there is no preposition *in*. We do not *believe in* the church, we *believe* the church and what the church professes in faith. In like manner, we do not *believe in* resurrection, but we *believe that there will be* a resurrection. The creed retains the preposition *in* for the persons of the godhead, I believe in the Father.... I believe in the Son.... I believe in the Holy Spirit.

Holy

To be holy has in some ways a pejorative sense in our culture. To call someone holy is not always a compliment. Think of "holy roller" or "holier than thou." Not many people strive to be *called* holy, even if they *strive for* holiness in their daily life. All too often it is saccharin piety that is deemed holy.

The term holy — *sanctus* in Latin, *hagios* in Greek, and *qadosh* in Hebrew — has as its root sense *to be set apart*. When used of persons, places, or things (and not God) the sense is that the person, place, or thing has been set apart for service to God.

When *holy* is used of God, it ultimately refers to God's otherness. The most famous example is found in the prophet Hosea, "For I am God and not a man, the Holy One present among you" (11:9b). Besides God, many other things are called holy in the Old Testament, including, for example, the land — we even refer to it today as the "Holy Land" — (Amos 7:17; Hosea 9:3; Ezekiel 4:12); priests (1 Chronicles 23:13; 2 Chronicles 23:6); vestments (Exodus 31:10); water (Numbers 5:17); oil (Numbers 35:25); and time, for example, a day (Nehemiah 8:9) or a Sabbath (Exodus 20:11). There are many such examples. Especially pertinent for our discussion is the fact that the people of God are called holy: "…you will be my treasured possession among all peoples, though all the earth is mine. You will be to me a kingdom of priests, a holy nation" (Exodus 19:5b-6a). Thus, the Old Testament concept of God clearly conveys that God is "other than" humanity, "other than" creation. God is set apart, yet intimately near ("among you" in Hosea 9:11). Persons, places, or things can also be set apart for service to God. Indeed the entire people of God is set apart for God as a treasured possession.

As we come to the New Testament, we might be surprised to find that the holiness of God is not often mentioned. In fact, only a few times is Jesus even called holy (Mark 1:24; Luke 1:35; 4:34; John 6:69; Acts 3:14; 4:27, 30; Revelation 3:7). Instead, the term *holy* is used most often to refer to the Christian people (for example, Acts 9:13; Philippians 4:22a), that is, the church (1 Corinthians 1:2; 2 Corinthians 1:1).[51] In fact, 1 Peter 2:9 quotes Exodus 19:6 (cited above) in what is believed to be a baptismal homily to Gentile converts.

> But you are "a chosen race, a royal priesthood, a holy nation, a people of his own, so that you may announce the praises" of him who called you out of darkness into his wonderful light. Once you were "no people" but now you are God's people; you "had not received mercy" but now you have received mercy (1 Peter 2:9-10).

In this way a holy church, a holy people, is that which is set apart from the world for God. The Vatican document *Lumen Gentium* (§ 9) quotes this same passage from 1 Peter in talking about the church. The early Christians were to be salt for the earth, the light of the world, a city set on a hill (Matthew 5:13-14). Thus *Lumen Gentium* speaks of the church's role in the world:

...all the faithful of Christ of whatever rank or status, are called to the fullness of the Christian life and to the perfection of charity; by this holiness as such a more human manner of living is promoted in this earthly society.... Furthermore, married couples and Christian parents should follow their own proper path (to holiness) by faithful love.... In this manner, they offer all (people) the example of unwearying and generous love; in this way they build up the brotherhood of charity; in so doing, they stand as the witnesses and cooperators in the fruitfulness of Holy Mother Church; by such lives, they are a sign and a participation in that very love, with which Christ loved his Bride and for which he delivered himself up for her. A like example, but one given in a different way, is that offered by widows and single people, who are able to make great contributions toward holiness and apostolic endeavor in the Church. Finally, those who engage in labor — and frequently it is of a heavy nature — should better themselves by their human labors. They should be of aid to their fellow citizens. They should raise all of society, and even creation itself, to a better mode of existence. Indeed, they should imitate by their lively charity, in their joyous hope and by their voluntary sharing of each others' burdens, the very Christ who plied his hands with carpenter's tools and who in union with his Father, is continually working for the salvation of all.... In this, then, their daily work they should climb to the heights of holiness and apostolic activity.[52]

Thus, Christians today, especially Catholics, are still called to be salt for the earth, to raise all of society to a better mode of existence. It is not enough, and in fact it is inadequate, simply to critique the world. Christians are called to transform it by our thoughts and actions, to build a more just society. Perhaps Pope Paul VI said it most succinctly: "if you want peace, work for justice."

Catholic

When the Apostles' Creed mentions the *catholic* Church, it means not so much the *Roman Catholic Church* but the *universal church*. The Greek term *katholikos* simply means universal. The early Christians realized that their local church was part of something bigger, more universal. These churches did not exist in isolation from one another but held common beliefs and practices that united them as one universal (catholic) church.

Even so, the term *catholic* as used in this article has been understood by many to refer primarily to the Roman Catholic Church. For example, this is the one word that Martin Luther changed in the Apostles' Creed. In fact, he changed this word to "Christian" so that in his Apostles' Creed the phrase read, "the holy Christian church, the communion of saints."[53]

Church

The word *church* in Greek is *ekklēsia*, which means "an assembly," or "those called out" (from the Greek *ek*, meaning "out," and *kaleō*, meaning "call" or "choose"). Though there is a universal sense to the church, as we saw above, there is also particularity.

For example, though Paul can speak of the churches of God in Judea (1 Thessalonians 2:15; Galatians 1:22), he also speaks of the church of God in Corinth (1 Corinthians 1:2; 2 Corinthians 2:1). Especially in 1 Corinthians, the sense of unity gained in partaking of the one cup and one bread is more than that of an individual church:

ANCIENT FAITH FOR THE MODERN WORLD

The cup of blessing that we bless, is it not a participation in the blood of Christ? The bread that we break, is it not a participation in the body of Christ? Because the loaf of bread is one, we, though many, are one body, for we all partake of the one loaf (1 Corinthians 10:16-17).

Moreover, Paul concludes chapter 10 of 1 Corinthians with an appeal for the Corinthians to "avoid giving offense, whether to Jews or Greeks or the church of God" (1 Corinthians 10:22). Shortly thereafter Paul claims that "you are the Christ's body, and individually parts of it" (1 Corinthians 12:27).

In Colossians and Ephesians, which were written later than 1 Corinthians, we can discern a development of Pauline ecclesiology. No longer do Christians make up the entire body of Christ, but here Christ "is the head of the body, the church" (Colossians 1:18; cf. Ephesians 5:23). The Christians make up the body, with Christ as its head. Christ is the principle of unity. Thus, the Colossian/Ephesian letters develop the ecclesiology we find earlier in Paul.

The marks of unity held by the church are outlined in Ephesians 4:4-6:

...one body and one Spirit, as you were also called to the one hope of your call; one Lord, one faith, one baptism; one God and Father of all, who is over all and through all and in all.

If we list these marks of unity by bullet point, we immediately see that there are seven:

- one body
- one Spirit

- one hope
- one Lord
- one faith
- one baptism
- one God and Father of all, who is over all
  and through all and in all

It is intriguing that "one Church" is not named or enumerated. The ecclesiological terminology is instead "one body." This Scripture passage has ramifications for ecumenical relations.

Today when a non-Catholic baptized Christian enters the Catholic Church, there is no need to "re-baptize." The Catholic Church recognizes the Baptism of other Christian traditions (Episcopalians, Methodists, Lutherans, etc.) In this way we are true to the ideal expressed in Ephesians 4:4-6; there is one Baptism.

Lumen Gentium (§8) said that the Church of Christ "subsists in" the Catholic Church. This represents a deepening and development of the doctrine of the church. The document does not say that the Church of Christ *is* the Catholic Church, but rather that Christ's Church *subsists in* the Catholic Church. This is to bring out "more clearly the fact that there are 'numerous elements of sanctification and of truth' which are found outside (the Catholic Church's) structure, but which 'as gifts properly belonging to the Church of Christ, impel towards Catholic Unity.'"[54]

So we see that the ecclesiological issues referred to in article nine of the Apostles' Creed are still very much alive and current.

Communion of Saints

As expressed in this article of the creed, the communion of saints makes up the church. When we speak of saints, we mean those canonized by the church, such as Mary, St. Francis of Assisi, St. Catherine of Siena, and St. Augustine, as well as the saints who have not been canonized, or officially declared so. For example, Paul addressed many of his letters to the "holy ones" or "saints." Often today *saint* has a pejorative sense. It is not a compliment to say of someone, "He thinks he's a saint." But in antiquity Paul exhorted his audience by reminding them that they were saints. Thus, they should act like it.

It is said that Dorothy Day did not want to be named a saint, because if she were she would no longer be perceived as "real." Saints are those whose images we revere in statues (marble or plastic) or on holy cards. However, it is important to realize that saints were and are real people who became upset, dealt with frustration, faced adversity and opposition, were mothers, fathers, priests, religious, royalty, and paupers. To be a saint is to exemplify the life of Christ in one's own life circumstances, including time and locale. We are not called to be third-century saints in the desert or twelfth-century saints in Medieval Europe, but twenty-first-century saints. What that looks like is up to us. Being a saint is not a privilege relegated to the special few but is the vocation of each and every person called by Christ in Baptism.

It is no accident that the creed refers to the *communion* of saints. Together, the saints who make up the church are themselves a community. Ours is not rugged individualism or a go-it-alone approach. For Christians, we are in this together, connected to all those who have come before us and all those who will come after us, but perhaps most importantly to all those who are with us now. Christians are to respect the common good and work with one another. Together, we are a holy community.

THE BOTTOM LINE

Those who profess this creed form a community of faith, a communion of saints. Together we are an assembly, an *ekklēsia*, a church that is both universal and particular. This community of believers is set apart from the world for service to God and one another in the world.

DISCUSSION QUESTIONS

Refer to Catechism of the Catholic Church, §748-975.

- In what ways does the Eucharist create unity in the church today? Give examples.

- Who are those that come to mind when you hear the word *saint*? What do you think of these people? How are you called in your own life to be a saint?

- Who is your favorite saint? Why? Name some others.

- What would inter-Christian relations look like if we focused on the seven principles of unity found in Ephesians 4:4-6?

Article Ten

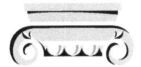

The forgiveness of sins...

Though "forgiveness of sins" in the tenth article of the Apostles' Creed is a hallmark of Christianity, its roots are in the Old Testament (Exodus 32:32; Leviticus 4:20; 5:6), where the term *sin* is often used in the sense of a debt or guilt incurred by having committed an offense. Thus, God's forgiveness of sin is the release of the perpetrator from the guilt and debt incurred by the offense.

Old Testament

In the example from Exodus cited above, Moses intercedes before God on behalf of the people, who had fashioned the golden calf at Aaron's instigation. Moses implores God, "If you would only forgive their sin!" (Exodus 32:32). In this story the Lord does not in fact forgive their sin but only punishes those who did sin. This fact actually marks a difference from other Old Testament punishments, such as that of Sodom and Gomorrah. In the Exodus story the people are not punished *collectively* but *individually*, based on their own committed actions.

In the book of Leviticus forgiveness of sin most often comes about through the ritual action of the Levitical priests. Sins were seen as debts incurred against God. Atonement could be made by a sacrifice proportionate to the sin that was committed. Certain sins required a greater sacrifice than others. For example, a sin of the community required the sacrifice of a bullock (Leviticus 4:13-21) whereas the sin of an individual person (not a priest or prince) required a she-goat or a lamb (Leviticus 4:27-35). Ritual impurity also required sin offering and holocaust (burnt offering) for atonement (for example, Leviticus 14:19-20).

The Day of Atonement was an annual day of fast and self-denial through which all Israel was cleansed of sin (Leviticus 16, especially 16:30). The ritual involved a blood sacrifice in the sanctuary and the sending away of the scapegoat, thereby banishing the sins of the people (Leviticus 16:20-22).

New Testament

These Old Testament images of atonement provided fertile ground for the imagination of early Christian thinkers. For example, the Letter to the Hebrews casts the salvific work of Jesus in terms of a heavenly Day of Atonement ceremony (Hebrews 6-9), with Jesus himself as high priest, offering his own blood.

Christianity is known for teaching the forgiveness of sin. The phrase *forgiveness of sins* or related variants occur throughout much of the New Testament, most notably in the Gospel of Luke and in Acts.[55] Of course, the term *forgiveness*, or *forgive*, also occurs quite often in the New Testament without modification. John the Baptist preaches a baptism of repentance for the forgiveness of sins (Luke 3:3). Jesus forgives sins (Luke 5:20), and in Luke we hear Jesus' words from the cross, "Father, forgive them, they know not what they do" (Luke 23:34). The Risen Lord commissions the disciples to forgive sins (Luke 24:47). The Lucan theme of forgiveness extends throughout the gospel and into the Acts of the Apostles (2:38; 5:31; 10:43; 13:38; 26:18).

We probably think we intuitively know what forgiveness of sins means. But what exactly does Luke mean by the term? The Greek term Luke uses for *forgiveness* is *aphesis*, which in layman's speech of the day most often was used in terms of cancellation of debt. Therefore, the expression "the power to forgive sin" refers to the power to release human beings from their debts (sins) before God.

This call for God to forgive sins is seen also in the Lord's Prayer, preserved for us both in Matthew and in Luke. Though it is Matthew's version of the prayer that Christians have memorized for centuries, it is worthwhile to compare the two versions.

ANCIENT FAITH FOR THE MODERN WORLD

Matthew 6:9b-13	Luke 11:2b-4
Our Father in heaven, hallowed be your name, your kingdom come, your will be done, on earth as in heaven. Give us today our daily bread; and forgive us our debts, as we forgive our debtors; and do not subject us to the final test, but deliver us from the evil one.	Father, hallowed be your name, your kingdom come. Give us each day our daily bread and forgive us our sins for we ourselves forgive everyone in debt to us, and do not subject us to the final test.

The Catholic biblical scholar, John P. Meier, has an excellent discussion of the Our Father and its historicity in volume two of *A Marginal Jew*.[56] In that book, Meier analyzes the differences between the Matthean and Lucan versions of the prayer to find that Matthew's version of the prayer reflects a liturgical setting, while Luke's version is more grounded in present-day concerns.

By carefully discerning what Matthew and Luke may have each contributed to the prayer, Meier postulates an original Aramaic form of the prayer going back to the historical Jesus and his loose band of followers, translated as:

Father,
hallowed be your name.
Your Kingdom come.
Our daily bread give us today.
And forgive us our debts
   as we forgive our debtors.
And do not lead us to the test.[57]

Thus, Jesus himself most likely taught the early disciples to forgive "debts" just as they (we) forgive those in debt to us. Much of the New Testament expresses an expectation of the imminent judgment of God upon the world. God's forgiveness in effect exempts one from that fearful day, although in this prayer Jesus offers us a troubling thought: Our forgiveness of others will determine God's forgiveness of us. This concept can be difficult or even troublesome for the modern believer who has been told that God forgives all, reconciles all, calls all. However, as Jesus would have it in the Lord's Prayer, even disciples may not be forgiven if they do not forgive others.

To make the point clear, immediately following the Lord's Prayer in the Gospel of Matthew, Jesus issues this promise:

> If you forgive others their transgressions, your heavenly Father will forgive you. But if you do not forgive others, neither will your Father forgive your transgressions (Matthew 6:14-15).

This somewhat troubling idea is not limited to the Lord's Prayer but finds an echo in many New Testament parables. For example, the Gospel of Matthew records the parable of aborted forgiveness in 18:23-35. In that story, a servant who owes much to the ruler is forgiven. The story says he owed ten thousand talents, which in that time was a fantastic amount that could never to be repaid. In fact, it would be like saying he owed millions and millions of dollars, the point being that he is not able to repay the money. The ruler in his kindness recognizes this and forgives the debt in its entirety. The released man turns around and demands a day's wages from another servant. When the ruler finds out, he does not mince words. "You wicked servant!" is his rebuke for the man, who is sent to the torturers until he pays back the entire debt. Jesus concludes by warning his disciples, "So will my heavenly Father do to you, unless each of you forgives his brother from his heart" (Matthew 18:35). The man who was released from his debt did not reciprocate. We are reminded that God's gracious act of mercy and forgiveness is to be emulated, not hoarded. God's forgiveness can in fact be revoked on the last day based on our own lack of forgiveness.

Other such stories in the New Testament include the story of the final judgment, again in the Gospel of Matthew (25:31-46). Here not everyone who cries "Lord, Lord" will be saved, but only those who do the will of the Father (7:21; 12:50). "For as you judge, so will you be judged, and the measure with which you measure will be measured out to you" (Matthew 7:2).

Luke echoes this thought with a slight variation:

Stop judging and you will not be judged. Stop condemning and you will not be condemned. Forgive and you will be forgiven. Give and gifts will be given to you; a good measure, packed together, shaken down, and overflowing, will be poured into your lap. For the measure with which you measure will in return be measured out to you (Luke 6:37-38).

Emulating the forgiveness that has been extended to us is a hallmark of Christianity and the basis of our salvation. The Gospel of John also has a strong theology of forgiveness of sins. Indeed, in John's resurrection appearance before the disciples, Jesus tells them: "Receive the holy Spirit. Whose sins you forgive are forgiven them, and whose sins you retain are retained" (John 20:22b-23). Though Jesus has conquered sin, the mission of the disciples is to forgive sins. In a sense, the disciples' vocation is now to forgive sins.

This mission or calling to forgive sins also finds attestation in the Letter of James, wherein the author reminds them, "...the prayer of faith will save the sick person, and the Lord will raise him up. If he has committed any sins, he will be forgiven. Therefore, confess your sins to one another and pray for one another, that you may be healed. The fervent prayer of a righteous person is very powerful" (James 5:15-16).

Certainly, the church celebrates the forgiveness of sins in the Sacrament of Reconciliation when the priest says, according to the Rite, "God, the Father of mercies, through the death and resurrection of his Son has reconciled the world to himself and sent the Holy Spirit among us for the forgiveness of sins; through the ministry of the Church may God give you pardon and peace, and I absolve you from your sins in the name of the Father, and of the Son, and of the Holy Spirit."

Forgiving sins happens not only in the confessional but each day, as the passage from James would indicate. When we think about this in terms of our own lives, much healing may happen when we step up to someone we have hurt and simply say, "I'm sorry. Please forgive me." The church also teaches that forgiveness for daily faults (venial/lesser sins) also occurs by reception of the Eucharist (CCC §1436).

In the early church, forgiveness of sins was one way of expressing and doing for oneself what God had done for humanity in Christ. At times it was said that our debts were forgiven, though this refers to a metaphorical rather than a literal debt. It is as though humanity, because of its collective sin, owed a debt to God that it could not pay. God responded with the Christ, who cancelled the debt, or paid it on our behalf. Some theologians queried to whom the debt was paid, but this is taking the metaphor too far. The point is that sins have been forgiven because of Christ. Now, individual Christians are to continue the effects of this cosmic event by confessing sins to one another and forgiving one another.

THE BOTTOM LINE

Forgiving sins is the mission of the church on earth (John 20:23). Christians are to be known for their forgiveness. In the end, our forgiveness of others will be the measure with which we are forgiven.

DISCUSSION QUESTIONS

Refer to *Catechism of the Catholic Church,* §976-987

- When is the last time you truly apologized to someone you hurt and asked for forgiveness? Tell the story, if you can.

- What kind of forgiveness can you expect from God given the amount of forgiveness you have shown others thus far? Explain.

Article Eleven

The resurrection of the body...

This eleventh article of the Apostles' Creed is based on Jesus' being raised, inasmuch as Christ is the "firstfruits of those who have fallen asleep" (1 Corinthians 15:20). That is, what happened to Christ will happen to us. So when Christians proclaim the resurrection of the body, we are proclaiming belief in our own resurrection from the dead. This belief in resurrection set Christians apart from most other religions in antiquity, yet it was an expression of an Old Testament belief, punctuated certainly by the resurrection of Jesus.

We recall that there are Old Testament stories of the dead being raised to life. For example, Elijah raised the widow's son in 1 Kings 17:17-24 and Elisha raised the Shunammite woman's son in 2 Kings 4:8-37. Even in the New Testament there are stories of raising from the dead. Jesus raised Lazarus (John 11:38-44), the widow's son at Nain (Luke 7:11-15), and Jairus' daughter (Matthew 9:18-19, 23-25; Mark 5:22-24, 35-43; Luke 8:41-42,49-56). Even Peter and Paul are said to have raised the dead (Acts 9:36-42; 20:7-12).

The belief in the resurrection of the body has been a standard of Christian faith for centuries. However, the manner in which this article of faith has been articulated has differed. For example, the Nicene Creed proclaims a belief in the resurrection of the dead. This wording is closer to the biblical text, since nowhere in the New Testament does the phrase *resurrection of the body* occur. Instead, the term most often used is *resurrection of the dead* (for example, Matthew 22:31; Luke 20:35; Acts 4:2; 17:32; 23:6; 24:21; 26:23; Romans 1:4; 1 Corinthians 15:12,13,21,42; Hebrews 6:2; 1 Peter 1:3). The Easter proclamation was not, "the body of Jesus has risen!" It was "the Lord has truly been raised!" (Luke 24:34).

Resurrection

Resurrection itself is a Semitic concept, springing from an anthropological view of the human being as a unified whole. In Hebrew there is scarcely a distinct word for *body*, though there is a term for *corpse*. In the Old Testament the human being is generally portrayed as a single entity with different aspects including thoughts, feelings, will, desire, flesh, spirit, and heart. Thus, the world view that birthed the concept of resurrection understood it as a restoration of the whole person. Once a person dies, that person is completely and entirely dead, without hope of life. Death is permanent, but resurrection reverses that condition, and the dead person is brought to life in his or her totality.

This holistic anthropological view reflected in Hebrew differed from that of the Greek world, which saw the human being primarily in terms of body and soul. The soul was thought to be immortal and shed the body at death to live forever. The interaction of these differing conceptions of the human being brought about interesting developments in early Christian thought.

We can see evidence of this cross-cultural interaction in 1 Corinthians when Paul is asked, in reference to the resurrection, "with what kind of body will they come back?" (1 Corinthians 15:35). His answer is "You fool!" Paul continues, "What you sow is not brought to life unless it dies" (1 Corinthians 15:36). We can see here that, unlike his Greek-speaking interlocutor, Paul does not accept or assume a fundamental separation between the soul and the body. He does not even think of the human being in those categories. Further, when Paul goes on to speak of sowing and dying, he indicates that not only will the human being be raised but he or she will undergo a transformation. In saying so, Paul makes an analogy with the seed and the tree. What we "sow" as a seed is the body, the corpse. When God raises us to new life, he will do so in a manner that transforms us in a way we cannot imagine. This will happen in a blink of an eye. Flesh and blood, the body as it is now, will not inherit the kingdom. Instead, there must be a transformation (1 Corinthians 15:35-58).

This was the kind of resurrection that Paul preached to his audience, many of whom lived in a world without the hope of life after death (cf. 1 Thessalonians 4:13). Some early Christians — perhaps co-workers of Paul — proclaimed that the resurrection had already happened and that Christians already lived a life of resurrection. But Paul responded:

> Hymenaeus and Philetus...have deviated from the truth by saying that (the) resurrection has already taken place and are upsetting the faith of some (2 Timothy 2:17b-18).

Paul is clear in stating that the resurrection will be a future event for those who have died in Christ (1 Thessalonians 4:13-18).

Though Paul witnessed the risen Christ, he never directly describes the experience. We do find three passages wherein he makes reference to it: (God) "was pleased to reveal his Son to me" (Galatians 1:15-16; "Have I not seen Jesus our Lord?" (1 Corinthians 9:1); and "Last of all, as to one born abnormally, he appeared to me" (1 Corinthians 15:8). None of these examples comes close to Luke's three-fold description of Paul's encounter with the risen Lord on the road to Damascus (Acts 9, 22, 26). In fact, the reader of Paul's letters is left grasping for details of the encounter that Luke depicts so vividly. Paul is content to make reference to his encounter by means of these pithy statements.

Despite Paul's forceful teaching in 1 Corinthians 15, early Christians such as Justin Martyr (1 Apology 18-19) began to speak of the *resurrection of the body* and the *immortality of the soul*. No longer was resurrection a restoration of the whole person. Resurrection was now understood to be a raising up of the corpse to be united with the immortal soul, an idea that is not found in the New Testament. Instead of *body*, some theologians preferred the term *flesh* (for example, Irenaeus, *Adversus Haereses*, 5.14.1). Indeed, many early Christian creeds proclaim belief in the resurrection of the flesh. The teaching of the scholastic period about resurrection is summarized in one line of the Second General Council of Lyons (1274): "we believe also in the true resurrection of this flesh that we now bear" (DS §854).

Ultimately, resurrection is a core belief of Christianity. For if Christ has not been raised, our faith is in vain. As St. Paul proclaims:

> But if Christ is preached as raised from the dead, how can some among you say there is no resurrection of the dead? If there is no resurrection of the dead, then neither has Christ been raised. And if Christ has not been raised, then empty (too) is our preaching; empty, too, your faith. Then we are also false witnesses to God, because we testified against God that he raised Christ, whom he did not raise if in fact the dead are not raised. For if the dead are not raised, neither has Christ been raised, and if Christ has not been raised, your faith is vain; you are still in your sins (1 Corinthians 15:12-17).

Thus, if we do not proclaim resurrection, our faith is in vain. In fact, we may ask, were Christ not raised from the dead, would Christianity have developed? The disciples scattered after the crucifixion, fearing they were to die next. The resurrection of Christ transformed death, and even gave death meaning. "For the wages of sin is death but the gift of God is eternal life in Christ Jesus our Lord." (Romans 6:23). In the resurrection, Christ conquered death. Now, for Christians there is hope of a future life with Christ, as Paul says in 1 Thessalonians 4:17b: "Thus we [the dead and the living] shall always be with the Lord." Since Christ

ANCIENT FAITH FOR THE MODERN WORLD

was raised, Christians believe that we too will be raised, for Christ is the firstfruits of those who have died (1 Corinthians 15:20,23). Christ's resurrection is, as it were, a promise for us. What happened to Christ will happen to those who believe in him. Death is not the final state for the Christian.

Problems with Resurrection?

Today, many Christians still have problems with resurrection.[58] We hear questions such as, "What age will I be when I am raised?" "Will I be raised with a thirty-year-old body, a fifty-year-old body, a seventy-year-old body?" "What if my corpse was cremated? How does the flesh return?"

These questions have vexed theologians for centuries. It was Athenagoras who wrote the first Christian treatise specifically on this subject, aptly titled *De Resurrectione*, or *On Resurrection*. Since he makes no mention of Christ and does cite the pagan physician Galen, he probably addressed the work to non-Christians. In it he discusses crass, physical problems associated with resurrection. For example, if a human being consumes an animal which itself had consumed a human being, how will God keep the parts straight at the resurrection (*De Resurrectione*, 4)? This was referred to as the "chain consumption argument." His answer basically consisted in the claim that this task would not be difficult for God, the creator of the world (*De Resurrectione*, 2-3;9). The resurrected bodies would in fact be made of reconstituted parts from their earthly bodies (*De Resurrectione*, 7). This led later theologians to wonder whether God might use one's former arm to make that same one's resurrected leg, or whether a former arm would have to be resurrected as an arm.

When we proclaim a resurrection of the flesh or resurrection of the body, the question often comes back to a variation of the famous chain consumption argument. Or we delve into questions that created theological problems regarding hair, blood, sweat, aborted fetuses; at what age we would appear; whether we would be handsome or ugly, husky or slim, male or female. Ultimately, these are not the questions that contribute to the profundity of the resurrection; rather, they drag it into the mire of the ridiculous, as Jerome himself experienced:

> And to those of us who ask whether the resurrection will exhibit from its former condition hair and teeth, the chest and the stomach, hands and feet, and other joints, then, no longer able to contain themselves and their jollity, they burst out laughing and adding insult to injury they ask if we shall need barbers, and cakes, and doctors, and cobblers, and whether we believe that the genitalia of which sex would rise, whether our (men's) cheeks would rise rough, while women's would be soft and whether the bodies would be differentiated based on sex. Because, if we surrender this point, they immediately proceed to female genitalia and everything else in and around the womb. They deny that singular members of the body rise, but the body, which is constituted from members, they say rises (*Epistula* 84.5).

Today we have a better understanding of biology and the created world than they did in antiquity. We know that our bodies regenerate nearly every single cell in seven years or so. I am literally not the same as I was ten years ago! Yet there is some fundamental identity that remains true. The early Christian thinker Origen approached this paradox when he referred to *river* as an appropriate name for the body (*Patrologia graeca*, 12. 1093). In doing so, he was attempting to hold together the two opposing concepts of identity and change. Though we say we are viewing the "same" river no matter what part of it we approach, in another way of course no river is the same from beginning to end; the various flotsam that it has picked up along the way, as well as the changing setting along the banks, can make one river very different at one end from the point at which it started. Additionally, if we simply stand on the bank of a river and watch it from that vantage point, we will see the river ebb, flow, and change. Yet it is the same river. Origen, however, was condemned by the church for some of his other views, and so ultimately it was the thinking of Jerome and Augustine, following Athenagoras in accenting the resurrection of this physical body, that would form the bedrock of Scholastic and later theology on the resurrection.

When we, like the Corinthians, ask, "with what sort of body will they come back," (1 Corinthians 15:35) we can hear Paul's answer still echoing from centuries ago, "You fool!" (1 Corinthians 15:36). What we sow is a bare kernel. It must be transformed. Flesh and blood shall not inherit the kingdom of God. As Christ is the firstfruits of the resurrection, what we say about Christ's resurrection dictates what we say about the general resurrection. Christ is no longer subject to death, for he has been raised to new life, seated at the right hand of God, exalted in glory.

It helps to remember that some of the most famous resurrection stories of the Old and New Testaments ended in subsequent death for those who were raised. That is, the widow's son raised by Elijah (1 Kings 17:17-24) and the Shunammite woman's son raised by Elisha (2 Kings 4:8-37) both subsequently died again. Likewise, Lazarus (John 11:38-44), the widow's son at Nain (Luke 7:11-15), and Jairus' daughter (Matthew 9:18-19, 23-25; Mark 5:22-24, 35-43; Luke 8:41-42, 49-56) — all raised from the dead by Jesus — died again at later times. Those raised from the dead by Peter and Paul (Acts 9:36-42; 20:7-12) died too. Too often we confuse resurrection of the body with a resurrection more akin to that of Lazarus than that of Jesus. We might refer instead to the resuscitation of Lazarus or the resuscitation of the widow's son from Nain.

For in calling these New Testament stories *resuscitation*, we are more accurately describing the theological import of the story.

Jesus, however, was not merely resuscitated. Jesus was raised from the dead to new life. His being raised was qualitatively different than the raising/resuscitation of Lazarus, or the raising/resuscitation of the widow's son from Nain. Jesus' resurrection may also be called exaltation, glorification, ascension, or seating at the right hand of God. In this way, when we claim that God raised Jesus from the dead, we are saying much more than that God simply resuscitated the crucified corpse of Jesus.

When in the Apostles' Creed we proclaim belief in the resurrection of the body, we are proclaiming that Christ is the firstfruits of the resurrection. We will share in the resurrection of Christ with everything it means to be human. We will not be disembodied souls, or revivified corpses, but resurrected human beings, raised to a new and glorious life with God and one another.

THE BOTTOM LINE

There is hope beyond death. Death does not mark an end but a change.[59] What happened to Jesus will happen to us. We will not be disembodied spirits but spiritual bodies (1 Corinthians 15:44). There will be a transformation from flesh and blood to something beyond our ability to describe (1 Corinthians 15:51-54).

DISCUSSION QUESTIONS

Refer to *Catechism of the Catholic Church,* §988-1019

- Discuss what the Catechism says about the resurrection of Christ.

- What do you believe will happen to you when you are raised from the dead? Describe it.

- How do you understand the human person — as a unity of body/soul or in some other way? Explain.

- Do you experience the power of the paschal mystery in your own life? Give examples.

Article Twelve

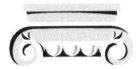

...and life everlasting. Amen.

The twelfth and final statement of the Apostles' Creed concerns the final destiny of believers, eternal life, a fundamental hope that can be found throughout all of humanity. The question that the rich man asks Jesus is perhaps the question asked by each individual human being. It concerns our final destiny, "Good Teacher, what must I do to inherit eternal life?" (Mark 10:17).

The idea of eternal life was expressed by some Greek thinkers using the term *immortal soul*. As we saw in the discussion of Article Eight on the Holy Spirit, Plato believed that at death a human being shed the body (the tomb of the soul). The immortal soul thus freed would live forever.

Old Testament

The Old Testament reflects a gradual awakening to the idea of everlasting life. In Genesis for example, Enoch is said not to have died but to have "walked with God" (Genesis 5:21-24). Other individuals are taken up as was Elijah, who "went up to heaven in a whirlwind (2 Kings 2:11). But despite a few unique examples, every other Old Testament figure died in one way or another. Everlasting life was not part of the belief system for the patriarchs and was non-existent throughout most of Old Testament times.

Some of the early ideas of eternal life were associated with offspring. That is, a person lived on through his or her descendants. This is one reason why it was so important to produce offspring. Other ideas concerning afterlife proposed *Sheol* or a shadowy, watery underworld one enters at death. The book of Jonah gives us a sense of this place:

> Out of my distress I called to the LORD, and he answered me; From the womb of Sheol I cried for help, and you heard my voice. You cast me into the deep, into the heart of the sea, and the

flood enveloped me; All your breakers and your billows passed over me. Then I said, "I am banished from your sight! How will I again look upon your holy temple?" The waters surged around me up to my neck; the deep enveloped me; seaweed wrapped around my head. I went down to the roots of the mountains; to the land whose bars closed behind me forever, but you brought my life up from the pit, O LORD, my God (Jonah 2:3-7).

Thus, *Sheol* serves as a poetic image for a pit of despair. *Sheol* was the realm of the dead, both good and bad. For example, the patriarch Jacob is said to be in *Sheol* (Genesis 37:35) as were Dathan and Abiram (Numbers 16). *Sheol* was the realm of the graves, the underworld. In this way, the Old Testament conformed with other ancient Near Eastern opinions on the afterlife. For example, extra-biblical literature from Ugarit, Egypt, and Mesopotamia confirms this sense of *Sheol* that we find in the Old Testament. So the Old Testament view simply reflects commonly held ideas of the time.

Not until the Book of Wisdom (about the second century B.C.) do we see belief in immortality expressed more along the lines of Greek thought: "But the souls of the just are in the hand of God, and no torment shall touch them" (Wisdom 3:1). Even today, this reading from the book of Wisdom is proclaimed often at Catholic funerals. Thus, the soul of a human being at death is with God. The Book of Wisdom is one of the few Old Testament books to have been written in Greek. Moreover, it was written in Alexandria, Egypt, a center of Greek thought and learning of the day. Jewish thinkers in Alexandria, steeped in Greek thought, sought to convey their own theology in Greek philosophical categories. Thus, we can see that language about "souls of the just" occurs in a Greek book of the Old Testament. Furthermore, it was in Alexandria that the Jewish community translated their Hebrew Scriptures into Greek.

New Testament

We will not be surprised to see that the New Testament does not speak of the human being in terms of body and soul, even though it does express belief in life after death. Christian belief in life after death is informed by the Old Testament and ultimately by the exaltation of Christ. The raising of Christ gives the Christian an insight into life after death. Paul says that Christ is the firstfruits of the resurrection (1 Corinthians 15:20,23). Paul uses the image of resurrection because he is thoroughly immersed in the thought world of the Old Testament. He does not express any notion of the immortality of Christ's soul. What happened to Christ after death will happen to all those who believe in him. The early Christians, who were for the most part Jews, already had a belief in life after death due to their reading of the Hebrew Scriptures. Their experience of the exalted Christ informed that belief. They could then proclaim that exaltation in terms of resurrection, glorification, or seated at the right hand of God, all of which were expressions found in the Old Testament.

It is a fundamental Christian belief that life does not end with our time on earth. Instead, we are destined for a life with Christ, with God, as Paul reminds us, "Thus we shall always be with the Lord" (1 Thessalonians 4:17b). This belief is also expressed in parables. For example, at the conclusion of the parable of the final judgment in Matthew, Jesus says, "And these will go off to eternal punishment, but the righteous to eternal life" (Matthew 25:46).

Eternal life is also a primary theme in the Gospel of John. In a conversation with Nicodemus, Jesus says, "For God so loved the world that he gave his only Son, so that everyone who believes in him might not perish but might have eternal life" (John 3:16). Now this verse has become a popular placard in end zones at football games. Is it so popular because it expresses the kernel of the Gospel? If so, this kernel of the

Gospel does not express resurrection, but rather eternal life. There is something in the human being that wants to live forever. It is a shared hope, a common dream.

Significant for Catholics is that the Gospel of John later ties eternal life to the Eucharist:

> "I am the living bread that came down from heaven; whoever eats this bread will live forever; and the bread that I will give is my flesh for the life of the world."

> The Jews quarreled among themselves, saying, 'How can this man give us (his) flesh to eat?' Jesus said to them, "Amen, amen, I say to you, unless you eat the flesh of the Son of Man and drink his blood, you do not have life within you. Whoever eats my flesh and drinks my blood has eternal life, and I will raise him on the last day. For my flesh is true food, and my blood is true drink. Whoever eats my flesh and drinks my blood remains in me and I in him. Just as the living Father sent me and I have life because of the Father, so also the one who feeds on me will have life because of me. This is the bread that came down from heaven. Unlike your ancestors who ate and still died, whoever eats this bread will live forever" (John 6:51-58).

The Gospel of John indicates that Jesus is the Eternal Word of God made flesh (1:1,14), the incarnate Word of God. (The Latin word *carnis* means "flesh." Think of *carne* at a restaurant. To say *incarnate* is to say *enfleshed*.) The unchanging, eternal Word of God descends into the earthly realm and actually changes into, or becomes, flesh. The unchanging changes. The eternal becomes temporal. The spiritual becomes carnal. The immaterial becomes material. The Word becomes flesh.

ANCIENT FAITH FOR THE MODERN WORLD

How then do we appropriate to ourselves this "Word become flesh"? By listening to the word and consuming the flesh, which is the bread of life (John 6). This is a sacramental understanding. Indeed it is an early expression of Catholic sacramentality. Human beings live in the world where God encounters them, in all the world's physical, messy, dirty, changing, temporal ways. For the believer in Jesus, it is not enough to listen to the Word of God. The believer will also literally consume the bread of life, the incarnate (enfleshed) Word of God.

Early church fathers understood this relationship between eternal life and Eucharist. For example, in his major work, *Adversus Haereses* (*Against Heresies*), Irenaeus writes:

> For just as the bread that is from the earth, when it receives the invocation of God, is no longer common bread, but the Eucharist, consisting of two realities, earthly and heavenly, so also our bodies, receiving the Eucharist, no longer are corruptible, but have the hope of resurrection (*Adversus Haereses*, 4.18.5.; cf. 5.2.3).

Thus, the relationship between eternal life and reception of the Eucharist has been a matter of belief since apostolic times.

Eternal life is the promise of God made long ago (Titus 1:2). We find references to it throughout the New Testament in the gospels, Acts, letters, and even in Jude! (Matthew 19:29; Mark 10:30; Luke 18:30; John 3:15,16; 4:14, 36; 5:24; 6:27,40,47,54,68; 10:28; 12:25,50; 17:2,3; Acts 13:46,48; Romans 2:7; 5:21; 6:22,23; Galatians 6:8; 1 Timothy 1:16; 6:12; Titus 1:2; 3:7; 1 John 1:2; 2:25; 3:15: 5:11,13,20; Jude 1:21). The concept of eternal life is more easily grasped than that of resurrection of the flesh or resurrection of the body. Life eternal is, as we have said, a shared hope for humanity.

As a matter of fact, this twelfth article of the creed has seemed so innocuous that it has engendered little debate over the centuries, unlike the previous article on resurrection which had to be clarified by later councils. The same Council of Lyons (A.D. 1274), cited above as reflecting the summary of Scholastic thought, professes this belief about life everlasting in the same sentence as that of resurrection. The sentence reads, "…we believe also in the true resurrection of this flesh that we now bear, and eternal life."[60] Indeed, the final article of the creed is expressed in only these two words: eternal life.

So, this last article of the Apostles' Creed has generated little controversy through the centuries. Perhaps this is so precisely because it expresses a common hope shared by humanity. There seems to be something in the human condition that longs for eternal life. The Vatican II document *Gaudium et Spes* (§18) states as much in its section on the Mystery of Death:

> It is in the face of death that the riddle of human existence grows most acute. Not only (are humans) tormented by pain and by the advancing deterioration of (their) body, but even more so by a dread of perpetual extinction. (They) rightly follow the intuition of (their) heart when (they) abhor and repudiate the utter ruin and total disappearance of (their) own person. (They) rebel against death because (they) bear in (themselves) an eternal seed which cannot be reduced to sheer matter. All the endeavors of technology, though useful in the extreme, cannot calm (their) anxiety; for prolongation of biological life is unable to satisfy that desire for higher life which is inescapably lodged in (their) breast.[61]

For Christians, belief in eternal life is an article of faith. Ultimately, life has meaning and we are destined for eternity. That message needs

ANCIENT FAITH FOR THE MODERN WORLD

to be proclaimed today as ever before, when we face a "dictatorship of relativism" that seeks to strip ultimate meaning from human existence. Today, as in the days when St. Paul wrote to the Thessalonians, Christians are not to be like the rest of humanity who have no hope. It is this hope of being forever with the Lord that drives our baptismal call to proclaim the good news to those who are far off and to those who are near. The Lord has risen. Our destiny awaits!

THE BOTTOM LINE

Though this life on earth will end, the life to come with Christ will never end. "Eye has not seen, ear has not heard, nor has it even entered the human heart, what God has ready for those who love him" (1 Corinthians 2:9).

DISCUSSION QUESTIONS

Refer to *Catechism of the Catholic Church*, §1020-1060 and §1061-1065, which address *Amen*, the final word of the creed.

- What do you thinkis the relationship between eternal life and Eucharist?

- What do you believe happens at death? Be specific.

- Does the difference between resurrection of the body and life everlasting matter to you? Why?

Conclusion

Today the Apostles' Creed is heard primarily at children's liturgies or prayed at the beginning of the rosary. Whenever it is heard or prayed, it is good to step back and reflect on this ancient articulation of the faith. Though we now recognize that each apostle did not contribute one article, we see that in many respects the beliefs that the creed professes are apostolic in that they were foreshadowed in the Old Testament and found expression in the New Testament. It helps our understanding to examine what the authors of the New Testament and the early church meant when they expressed their faith in writing gospels, letters, creeds, and other documents. In so doing, we might come to a deeper understanding of our own faith.

The articles of the creed are perhaps more germane today than ever. Yet we understand that the entirety of our faith is not encapsulated in the Apostles' Creed, for there is no mention of Sacraments or even the Eucharist. There is no mention of liturgy, or communal prayer, or the Our Father. Still, the creed has a unique position in the life of the church. It reminds us of core beliefs, some stated in metaphorical images and others in concise statements, which can sometimes be forgotten.

In looking to refresh our knowledge of the faith, there is perhaps no better starting point than the Apostles' Creed.

APPENDIX A

Timeline

27/30	Death of Jesus
B.C. 20 – A.D. 50	Philo of Alexandria
64/67	Death of Peter and Paul
circa 95	1 Clement
circa 37 – 100	Josephus
circa 117	Death of Ignatius of Antioch
circa 69 – 155	Polycarp
circa 63 – 113	Pliny (the Younger)
reigned 98 – 117	Trajan (Roman Emperor)
circa 100 – 165	Justin Martyr
circa 110-160	Marcion
flourished 176 – 180	Athenagoras
circa 125 – 200	Irenaeus of Lyons
circa 150 – 216	Clement of Alexandria
circa 150 – 230	Tertullian
circa 185 – 254	Origen
died circa 240	Hippolytus of Rome
325	Council of Nicea
circa 320 – 403	Epiphanius of Salamis
345 – 410	Rufinus
347 – 420	Jerome
354 – 430	Augustine
1225 – 1274	Thomas Aquinas
1274	Second General Council of Lyons
1483 – 1546	Martin Luther

1545 – 1563 Council of Trent
        1566 Roman Catechism
1962 – 1965 Vatican II
1964 – 1978 Pontificate of Paul VI
1978 – 2005 Pontificate of John Paul II
        1992 *Catechism of the Catholic Church*, first edition
        1997 *Catechism of the Catholic Church*, second edition
2005 – 2013 Pontificate of Benedict XVI
        2006 United States Catholic Catechism for Adults
      2013 – Pontificate of Francis

ANCIENT FAITH FOR THE MODERN WORLD

APPENDIX B

Apostles' Creed and Nicene Creed

Apostles' Creed

I believe in God,
the Father almighty,
Creator of heaven and earth,
and in Jesus Christ, his only Son, our Lord.
who was conceived by the power of the Holy Spirit
born of the Virgin Mary,
suffered under Pontius Pilate,
was crucified, died, and was buried;
he descended into hell;
on the third day he rose again;
he ascended into heaven,
and is seated at the right hand of the Father;
from there he will come to judge the living and the dead.

I believe in the Holy Spirit,
the holy catholic Church,
the communion of saints,
the forgiveness of sins,
the resurrection of the body,
and life everlasting.
Amen.

Nicene Creed

I believe in one God,
the Father almighty,
maker of heaven and earth,
of all things visible and invisible.

I believe in one Lord Jesus Christ,
the Only Begotten Son of God,
born of the Father before all ages.
God from God, Light from Light,
true God from true God,
begotten, not made, consubstantial with the Father;
through him all things were made.
For us men and for our salvation
he came down from heaven,
and by the Holy Spirit was incarnate of the Virgin Mary,
and became man.
For our sake he was crucified under Pontius Pilate,
he suffered death and was buried,
and rose again on the third day
in accordance with the Scriptures.
He ascended into heaven
and is seated at the right hand of the Father.
He will come again in glory
to judge the living and the dead
and his kingdom will have no end.

I believe in the Holy Spirit, the Lord, the giver of life,
who proceeds from the Father and the Son,
who with the Father and the Son is adored and glorified,
who has spoken through the prophets.

I believe in one, holy, catholic and apostolic Church.
I confess one Baptism for the forgiveness of sins
and I look forward to the resurrection of the dead
and the life of the world to come.
Amen.

NOTES

Introduction

1. This legend has its roots in Sermon 240 of Augustine, which is now considered to have been written in the ninth century A.D. and falsely attributed to Augustine. See J.N.D. Kelly, *Early Church Creeds*. (Singapore: Longman, 1972), 3.

2. Ignatius, "To the Trallians" 9, in *The Apostolic Fathers*, Loeb Classical Library, Vol. 1. (Cambridge, MA: Harvard University Press, 2003).

3. "Canons of Hippolytus" text of Hippolytus' Apostolic Tradition, 21.9-18 in Bradshaw, Paul F., M.E. Johnson, and L. Edward Phillips. *The Apostolic Tradition. Hermeneia.* (Minneapolis, MN: Fortress, 2002), 115, 117, 119.

4 J.N.D. Kelly, *Rufinus: A Commentary on the Apostles' Creed, Ancient Christian Writers*, 20: (Westminster, MD: Newman Press, 1955), 15-16.

5. I am following here the first chapter of *Early Church Creeds*. The reader is directed to that study to find a more thorough treatment of the subject matter.

6. Cf. Martin Luther's *Smaller Catechism, Larger Catechism*, and various sermons, e.g, *Luther's Works*, 51.166 (St. Louis: Concordia Publishing House, 1955).

Article One

7. The term *kyrios* translates the tetragrammaton only in such Septuagint manuscripts as were copied by Christian scribes. It has been shown that *kyrios*, *adôn*, and *mare* were all used by pre-Christian Palestinian Jews for Yahweh. See J.A. Fitzmyer, "New Testament *Kyrios* and *Maranatha* and their Aramaic Background," in *To Advance the Gospel.* (Grand Rapids, MI: W.B. Eerdmans: 1998), 220-23.

8. E.g., Elizabeth Johnson, *She Who Is* (Tenth Anniversary Edition). New York: Herder & Herder, 2002. Catherine M. Lacugna, *Freeing Theology: The Essentials of Theology in Feminist Perspective.* New York: HarperOne, 1993.

Article Two

9. Fitzmyer, Romans, *Anchor Bible 33* (New York: Doubleday, 1993), 111; J.P.Meier, A Marginal Jew, vol. 1 (New York: Doubleday, 1991), 205-208.

10. Many times people ask why we don't call Jesus Josh or Joshua? The Latin translation of the Greek name is *Iesus*. In the late middle ages, the consonantal "i" (that is, when "i" precedes a consonant and is pronounced like a "y") came to be rendered with the "j" sound. Thus, we say *Jesus* even though a direct translation of the name from Hebrew could and would yield *Josh*.

11. The term *messiah* has a "rubber band extension" quality to it, to borrow J. A. Fitzmyer's term in "Qumran Messianism," in *The Dead Sea Scrolls and Christian Origins* (Grand Rapids, MI: W.B. Eerdmans,), 73. Both he, in the article cited above, and J. H. Charlesworth (*The Messiah: Developments in Earliest Judaism and Christianity: The First Princeton Symposium on Judaism and*

Christian Origins. Minneapolis, MN: Fortress, 1992) give a good sense of the problem, namely, the slippery nature of the use of this title. More recently, there is J. Fitzmyer, *The One Who Is To Come*. (Grand Rapids, MI: W.B. Eerdmans, 2007).

12. The Pontifical Biblical Commission, *The Jewish People and Their Sacred Scriptures in the Christian Bible*, 2002, §21, accessed April 06, 2015, http://www.vatican.va/roman_curia/congregations/cfaith/pcb_documents/rc_con_cfaith_doc_20020212_popolo-ebraico_en.html.

13. Letter (X.25 ff) from Pliny to the Emperor Trajan (about 112 A.D.).

14. Chapter 20 was the original conclusion of the gospel. What editors call "the epilogue" (chapter 21) was added later. For more on this see R.E. Brown, *The Gospel of John. Anchor Bible 29, 29A*. 2 vols. (New York: Doubleday, 1966).

Article Three

15. Though the Gospel of John mentions Jesus' mother, she is never named (John 2:1,3,5,12; 6:42; 19:25,26). We need the Synoptic Gospels and Acts (e.g., Acts 1:14) to know that the name of Jesus' mother was Mary.

16. Ignatius, "Letter to the Ephesians" 7, in *The Apostolic Fathers: Greek Texts and English Translations*, trans. Michael W. Holmes (Grand Rapids: MI; Baker, 1999).

17. W. R. Schoedel, *Ignatius of Antioch: A Commentary on the Letters of Ignatius of Antioch* (Hermeneia; Philadelphia: Fortress, 1985), 20.

Article Four

18. Though Josephus, the gospels, and Tacitus refer to Pilate as a Procurator, the recently (1961) discovered Pilate Stone in Caesarea Maritima makes clear that Pilate was a Prefect. cf. Josephus, *Jewish Wars* 2.169-177, Loeb Classic Library, Vol. 1 (Cambridge, MA: Harvard University Press, 1997); Josephus, *Jewish Antiquities* 18.55-59, 62, 85-87, Loeb Classic Library, vol. 8 (Cambridge, MA: Harvard University Press, 1998); Philo, *On the Embassy to Gaius*, General Indexes 299-302, Loeb Classic Library (Cambridge, MA: Harvard University Press, 1962).

19. Fitzmyer, J. Acts. *Anchor Bible 31*. (New York: Doubleday, 1998) 391.

20. Josephus, *Jewish Antiquities* 18.4.2; Philo, *Embassy to Gaius*, 38.

21. Pontifical Biblical Commission, *The Jewish People and their Sacred Scriptures*, §71.

22. Appian, *Roman History*, Volume III: The Civil Wars 1.120, Loeb Classic Library (Cambridge, MA: Harvard University Press, 1913).

23. For more on this important issue, see J. Fitzmyer. *The One Who Is To Come*. (Grand Rapids, MI: W.B. Eerdmans, 2007).

24 There are many studies on the life and chronology of Paul. A sketch of his life can be found in the article "Paul" §79 in the *The New Jerome Biblical Commentary*. (Englewood Cliffs, N.J.: Prentice-Hall, 1990). A more detailed study can be found in J. Murphy-O'Connor. *Paul: A Critical Life*. (Oxford: New York, 1996).

25. Susan Jacoby, "The Theodicy Problem: No Problem for An Atheist — OnFaith," *On Faith*, September 05, 2007, accessed April 01, 2015, http://www.faithstreet.com/onfaith/2007/09/05/the-theodicy-problem-no-proble/5275.

Article Five

26. Ephesians 4:9 speaks of a descent into the lower regions of the earth, but this is not the inferna.

27. Rufinus, *A Commentary on the Apostles' Creed* §18 in *Ancient Christian Writers* 20.52 (trans. J.N.D. Kelly).

28. The term *gehenna* is found in twelve places in the New Testament: Matthew 5:22,29,30; 10:28; 18:9 23:15,33; Mark 9:43,45,47; Luke 12:5; James 3:6.

29. "Gehenna" 2, in *Anchor Bible Dictionary,* ed. David Noel Freedman (New York: Doubleday, 1992).

30. J. E. Elliott. 1 Peter. *Anchor Bible 37B.* (New York: Doubleday, 2000), 709, cf. 706-710.

31. Pope John Paul II (General Audience, January 11, 1989), accessed April 6, 2015, http://w2.vatican.va/content/john-paul-ii/it/audiences/1989/documents/hf_jp-ii_aud_19890111.html.. Available online in Italian and Spanish. Translation here is my own from the Italian.

32. *United States Catholic Catechism for Adults.* (Washington, DC: United States Conference of Catholic Bishops, 2006), 93.

Article Six

33. For example, the Ancient Greeks knew roughly the circumference of the earth. They reasoned that if the earth were rotating on its axis, it would make one complete 24,000 mile rotation in 24 hours. In other words, if the earth were rotating on its axis everything on the earth would be traveling at about 1,000 miles/hour. If that were the case, why do we not simply spin off the earth? How would birds fly against a thousand mile per hour wind? Wouldn't clouds simply dissipate or become wispy bands across the sky?

Furthermore, if the earth were rotating on its own axis, it would necessarily be revolving around the sun. The Greeks estimated the distance of the earth to the sun at millions of miles (the actual distance being about 93 million miles). Six months later, the earth is millions of miles away from where it was six months earlier (about 186 million miles as we now know). Still, on any given night the stars appear in certain locations. Why don't the stars appear to be in different locations with respect to one another as the earth is moving millions of miles back and forth every six months? And how fast would the earth need to travel to get back and forth every six months? Rotation on its axis at 1,000 miles per hour and revolution around the sun at speeds even greater than that, combined to create an incredibly violent and fantastic image of the earth's movement that was too much for the ancient Greeks to accept.

Also, if the stars are so far away, how can we see them at all? They would have to be incredibly bright, and unbelievable large to shine so brightly that we would see them at all. So in fact, the ancients had good reasons for deducing that the earth was a stationary sphere, and that the stars, moon, and sun moved around it.

And yet, in spite of their clear logic, the Ancient Greeks were wrong. The earth does rotate on its axis and it does revolve around the sun. Gravity (unknown to the Ancient Greeks) explains why things do not fly off the earth when the earth is moving at such incredible speeds. And the Greeks were actually correct about the issue of the stars' position in the night sky relative to the earth's position (known today as stellar parallax). The stars are in fact so far away (much further than the Greeks imagined) that there is only a miniscule degree of stellar parallax. Such precise instruments designed to measure the infinitesimal degree of stellar parallax was not invented until the nineteenth century.

Article Seven

34. Paul's concept of judgment is complicated. At times he speaks of God judging outsiders (1 Corinthians 5:13). At other times he speaks of the saints or holy ones judging the world and the angels (1 Corinthians 6:2-3). In some sense we are listening in while the early Christians forge theology. Paul is reconciling traditional Jewish belief with his experience of the Risen Christ.

Article Eight

35. Cf. also Genesis 1:2.

36. E.g., Judges 3:10; 6:34; 11:29; 13:25; 14:6,19; 15:14; 1 Samuel 10:6; 16:13-14; 2 Samuel 23:2; 1 Kings 22:24 = 2 Chronicles 18:23; Isaiah 11:2; 63:14; Ezekiel 11:5; Micah 3:8; 2 Chronicles 20:14; Isaiah 61:1.

37. Exodus 31:3; 35:31; Numbers 24:2; 1 Samuel 10:10; 11:16; 19:20,23; 2 Chronicles 15:1; 24:20.

38. Judges 3:10.

39. 1 Samuel 10:10; 19:23.

40. I am using here only the undisputed letters of Paul:

    Romans 1:4,9; 2:29; 5:5; 7:6; 8:2,4,5 (twice), 6,9 (three times),
    10,11 (twice), 13,14,15 (twice), 16 (twice), 23,26 (twice), 27; 9:1;
    11:8; 12:11; 14:17; 15:13,16,19,30

    1 Corinthians 2:4,10 (twice), 11 (twice), 12 (twice), 13,14; 3:16;
    4:21; 5:3,4,5; 6:11,17,19; 7:34, 40; 12:3 (twice), 4,7,8 (twice), 9
    (twice), 10,11, 13 (twice); 14:2,12,14,15 (twice), 16,32; 15:45;
    16:18

    2 Corinthians 1:22; 2:13; 3:3,6 (twice), 8,17 (twice),18; 4:13; 5:5;
    6:6; 7:1,13; 11:4; 12:18; 13:13

    Galatians 3:2,3,5,14; 4:6,29; 5:5,16,17 (twice), 18,22, 25 (twice);
    6:1,8 (twice),18

    Philippians 1:19,27; 2:1; 3:3; 4:23

    1 Thessalonians 1:5,6; 4:8; 5:19,23

    Philemon 1:25.

41. Romans 2:9; 11:3; 13:1; 16:4; 1 Corinthians 15:45; 2 Corinthians
    1:23; 12:15; Philippians 1:27; 2:30; 1 Thessalonians 2:8; 5:23.

42. Fitzmyer, Romans, 127. Paul uses *pneuma* in an anthropological
    sense to refer to that aspect of the person which is open to receive
    the Spirit of God, or the means by which a person relates most
    directly to God: "for God is my witness, whom I serve with my
    spirit by announcing the gospel of his Son, that without ceasing I
    remember you always in my prayers" (Romans 1:9). Later in the
    same letter Paul claims: "it is the Spirit itself bearing witness with
    our spirit that we are children of God" (Romans 8:16).

43. Scholars disagree as to whether Paul uses *Lord* in this verse to
    refer to Christ, as does Herman N. Ridderbos in *Paul: An Outline*

ANCIENT FAITH FOR THE MODERN WORLD

of His Theology (Grand Rapids, MI: W.B. Eerdmans, 1975), 87: or to "'the Lord' of the text just adapted," as does James D. G. Dunn in *The Theology of Paul the Apostle* (Grand Rapids, MI: W.B. Eerdmans, 1998), 422. Ridderbos cites 2 Corinthians 3:17 as an example where "Christ and the Spirit are placed in a certain relationship of identity with each other."

44. Eduard Schweizer, *"pneuma, pneumatikos"* 6, in *Theological Dictionary of the New Testament*, ed. Gerhard Kittel. (Grand Rapids, MI: W.B. Eerdmans, 1968).

45. The phrase *to pneuma tou anthrōpou to en autō(i)* (the human spirit within) serves as an example of *pneuma* referring to the innermost depths of a person.

46. "...yet we speak about wisdom to those who are mature, but not about a wisdom of this age, or even of the rulers of this age who are passing away" (1 Corinthians 2:6).

47. In Galatians 5:19b-21a, Paul lists examples of the works of the flesh: "illicit sexual union, fornication, uncleanness, licentiousness, idolatry, sorcery, hatred, strife, jealousy, wrath, quarrels, divisions, factions, envy, drunkenness, carousing and the like."

48. Though there is no Old Testament evidence to suggest a rivalry between Ishmael and Isaac, such a rivalry is referred to in later rabbinic sources.

49. F. J. Matera, Galatians, *Sacra Pagina 9*. (Collegeville, MN: Liturgical Press, 1992), 216.

50. *Rite of Baptism for Children*, §97, 148, et al. in *The Rites of the Catholic Church*. (New York: Pueblo Publishing, 1976).

Article Nine

51. The noun *hagios* is used 233 times in the New Testament. See Horst Bachmann et al., *Concordance to the Novum Testamentum Graece of Nestle-Aland,* 26th Edition, and to the Greek New Testament, 3rd Edition. (Berlin; New York: De Gruyter, 1987), 20-26.

52. Pope Paul VI, *Lumen Gentium, (Dogmatic Constitution on the Church*), November 21, 1964, §41, accessed April 06, 2015, http://www.vatican.va/archive/hist_councils/ii_vatican_council/documents/vat-ii_const_19641121_lumen-gentium_en.html.

53. Martin Luther, *The Large Catechism of Martin Luther*, ed. Robert H. Fischer (Radford, VA: Wilder Publishing, 1959), 10.

54. Congregation for the Doctrine of the Faith, "Responses to Some Questions Regarding Certain Aspects of the Doctrine on the Church," June 27, 2007, accessed April 06, 2015, http://www.vatican.va/roman_curia/congregations/cfaith/documents/rc_con_cfaith_doc_20070629_responsa-quaestiones_en.html.

Article Ten

55. Luke 1:77; 3:3; 24:47; Acts 2:38; 5:31; 10:43; 13:38; 26:18.

56. John P. Meier, *A Marginal Jew: Rethinking the Historical Jesus*, Vol. 2. (New York: Doubleday, 1994), 291-302.

57. Ibid., 292-293.

Article Eleven

58. E.g., Laura Sheahan writes an article questioning, "Why doesn't bodily resurrection interest, much less delight, people who are otherwise devout?" See "The Resurrection of the Body," *America*, 196, no. 12 (April 2, 2007), 20.

59. As the liturgy of the church states (*Roman Missal*, Preface of Christian Death I, also quoted in CCC §1012):

   Lord, for your faithful people life is changed, not ended.

   When the body of our earthly dwelling lies in death

   we gain an everlasting dwelling place in heaven.

Article Twelve

60. Denzinger, H., and Schönmetzer, A. *Enchiridion symbolorum definitionum et declarationum de rebus fidei et morum.* 35th Edition.

61. Taken from Pope Paul VI, *Gaudium Et Spes*, December 7, 1965, accessed April 06, 2015, http://www.vatican.va/archive/hist_councils/ii_vatican_council/documents/vat-ii_cons_19651207_gaudium-et-spes_en.html.

Acknowledgments

The first version of this book was published nearly a decade ago as *The Apostles' Creed: Articles of Faith for the Twenty-First Century*. It seems each year there are many events, talks, sessions, and lectures on this fundamental expression of Christian belief. This current edition has been revised in many instances for the sake of clarity and has been shaped by many adult education sessions and public lectures. There are also fewer footnotes. Since the time of the first edition, the liturgical texts we pray also have been updated. This revision has taken that into account as well.

This book would not be complete without gratitude expressed to Dr. Diana Dudoit Raiche, who first suggested this project to me over a decade ago. As fellow graduate students at The Catholic University of America, and now as colleagues in religious education, it would be an honor if some of her dynamic energy and vision for a more theologically informed laity were translated into these pages. My thanks also to Sarah Layli Sahrapour, a graduate assistant at Loyola University Chicago. She double-checked the source material, updated classical citations, and refreshed scriptural citations to conform to the *New American Bible, Revised Edition*. She gave the entire manuscript a fresh read and recommended many improvements. Aside from her editorial and proofreading help, her notes allowed me to rethink some things and to present ideas with more clarity. Anything unclear or not properly cited at this point is due solely to my own oversight. Deacon Denis Simon again generously sponsored me in making a Holy Week retreat with the Jesuits at Lake Dallas. That time of tranquility provided the opportunity to finish this revised manuscript.

Finally, thanks to Marnie, John, Clare, Peter, and Helen for their patience and understanding when duties keep me away from them.

Also Available

The Message: Catholic Ecumenical Edition
1,984 pages, paperback and hardcover

Explain THAT to Me!
Searching the Gospels for the Honest Trust about Jesus
Joseph McHugh • 108 pages, paperback

Getting to Know The Bible
An Introduction to Sacred Scripture for Catholics
Rev. Melvin Farrell, revised by Joseph McHugh • 112 pages paperback

Great Men of the Bible: A Guide for Guys
Rev. Martin Pable • 216 pages, paperback

Books by Alice Camille

This Transforming Word
Three Volumes: Cycles A, B, C
240-250 pages, paperback

God's Word Is Alive
416 pages, paperback

Invitation to the New Testament
102 pages, paperback

Invitation to the Old Testament
102 pages, paperback

Invitation to Catholicism
243 pages, paperback

Available from Booksellers Nationwide
or from ACTA Publications • 800-397-2282 • actapublications.com

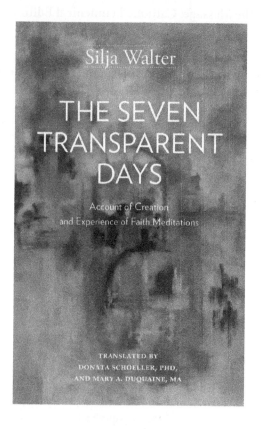